Happiness At The Tip Of My Pen
Book 1

Art.Z illustrations
Griswold Ct
ArtZillustrations.com

Created and Printed in the USA

Illustrations by Bonnie S. MacLachlan

ISBN 978-0-9970237-8-7

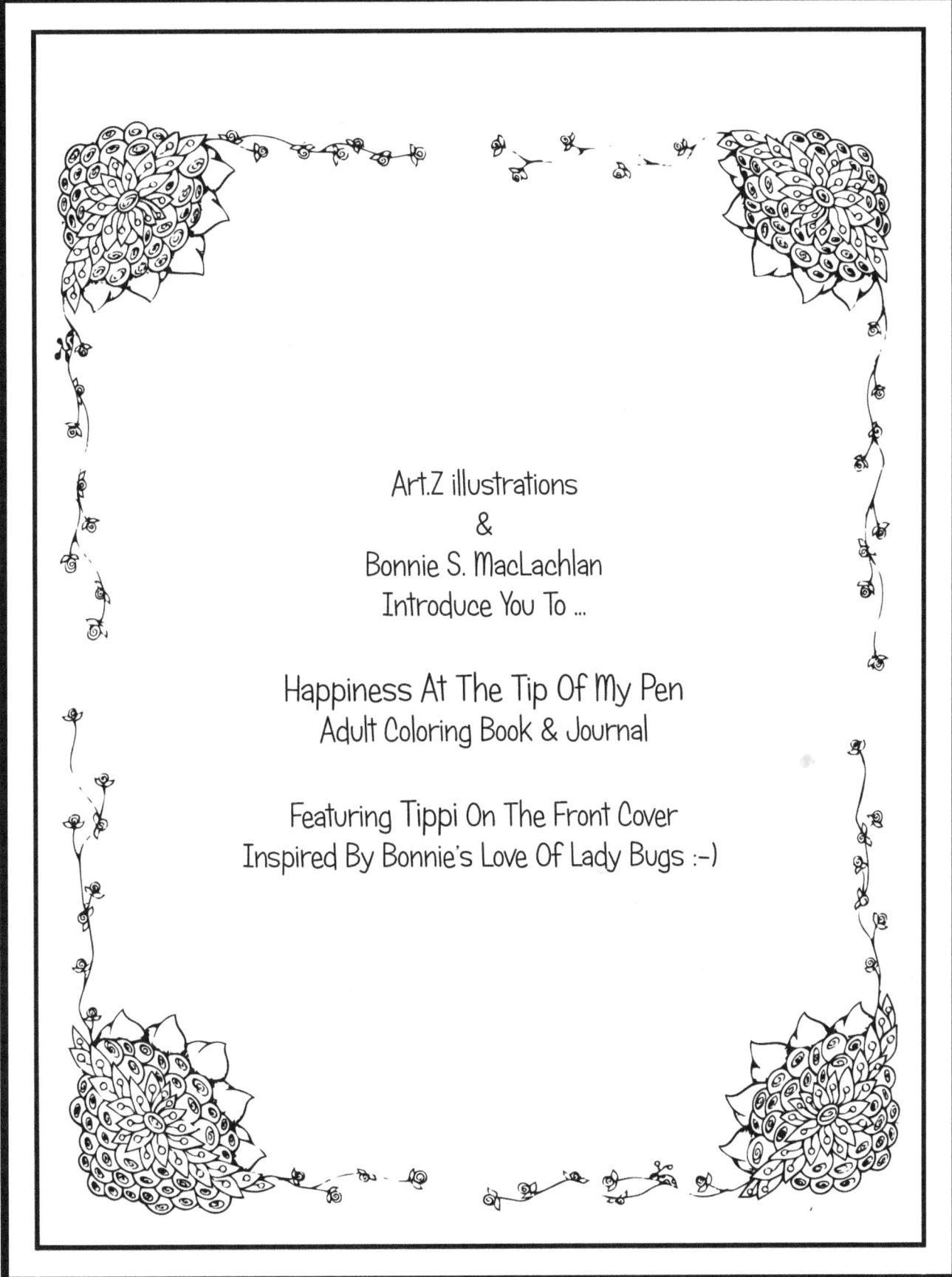

Art.Z illustrations
&
Bonnie S. MacLachlan
Introduce You To ...

Happiness At The Tip Of My Pen
Adult Coloring Book & Journal

Featuring Tippi On The Front Cover
Inspired By Bonnie's Love Of Lady Bugs :-)

www.ArtZillustrations.com

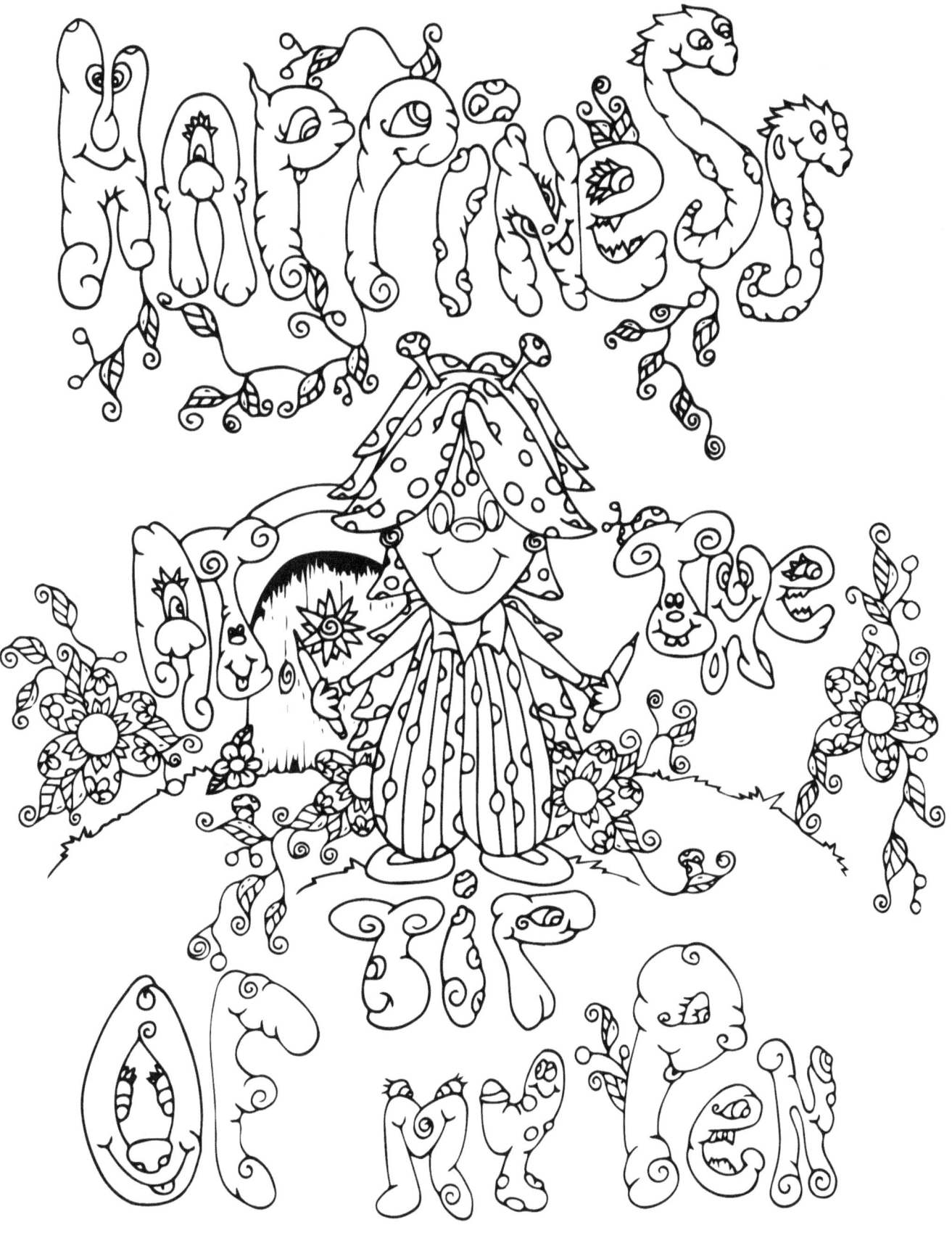

Happiness Lives at the Tip of My Pen

This Book Belongs To _____

www.ArtZillustrations.com

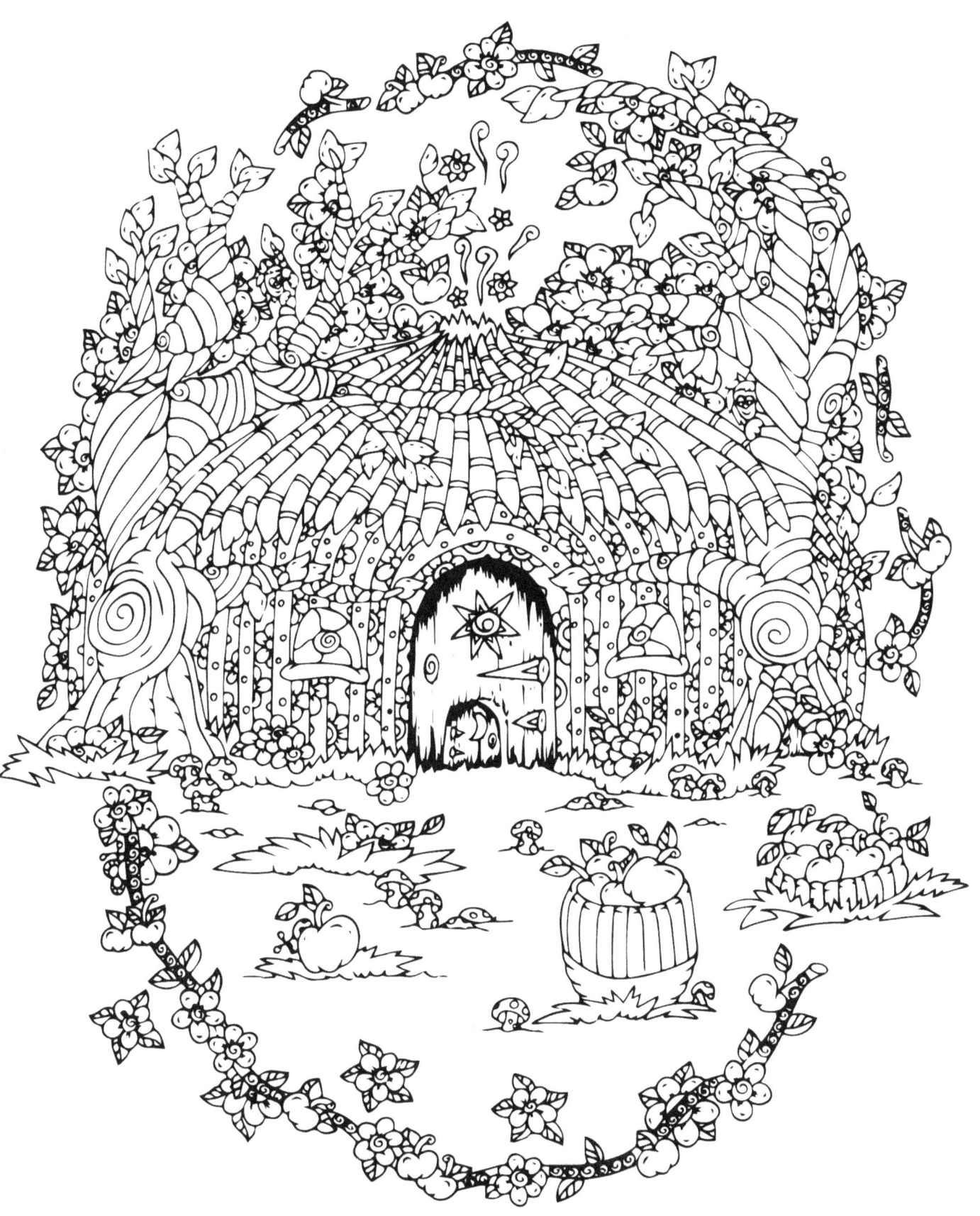

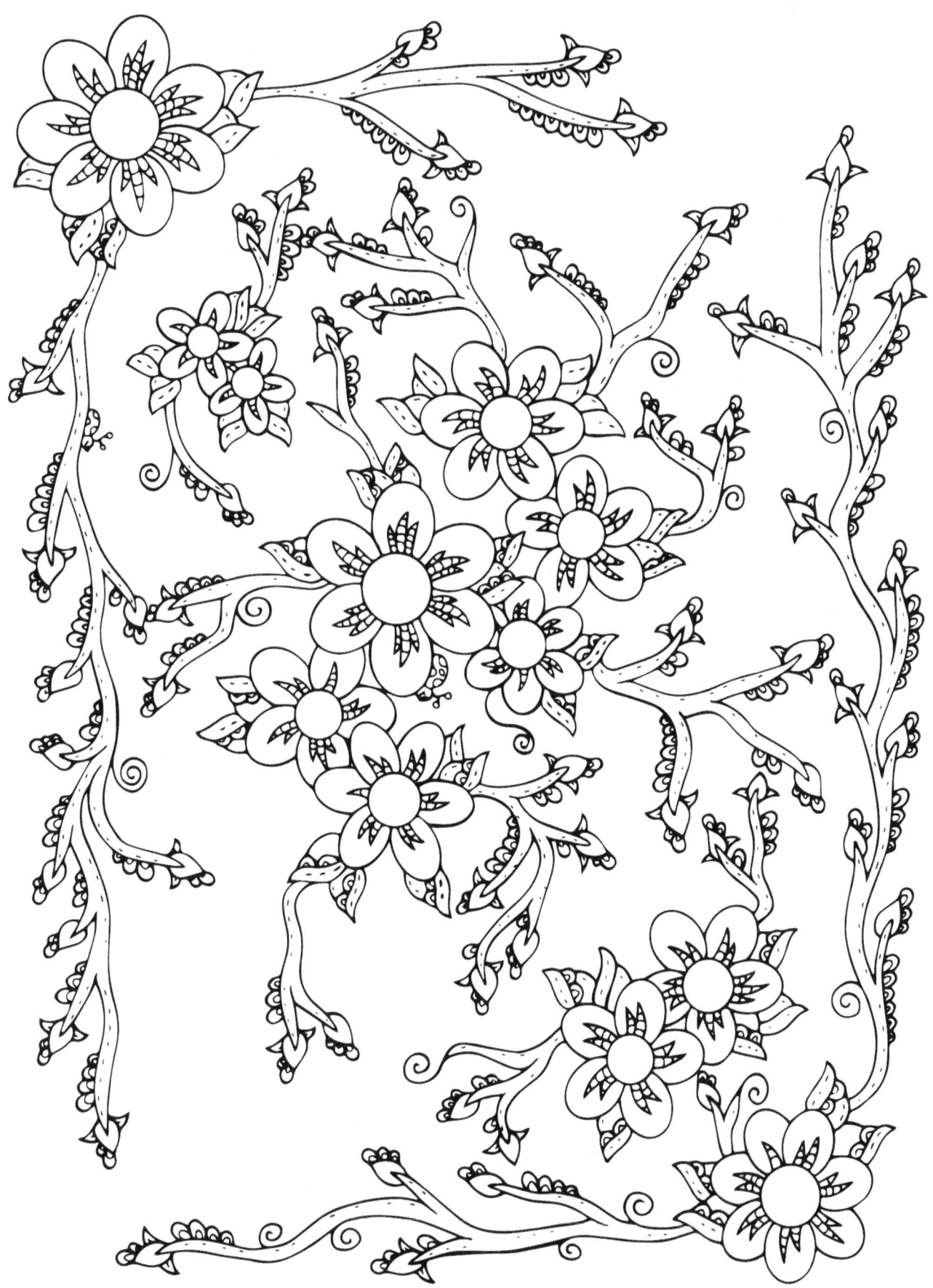

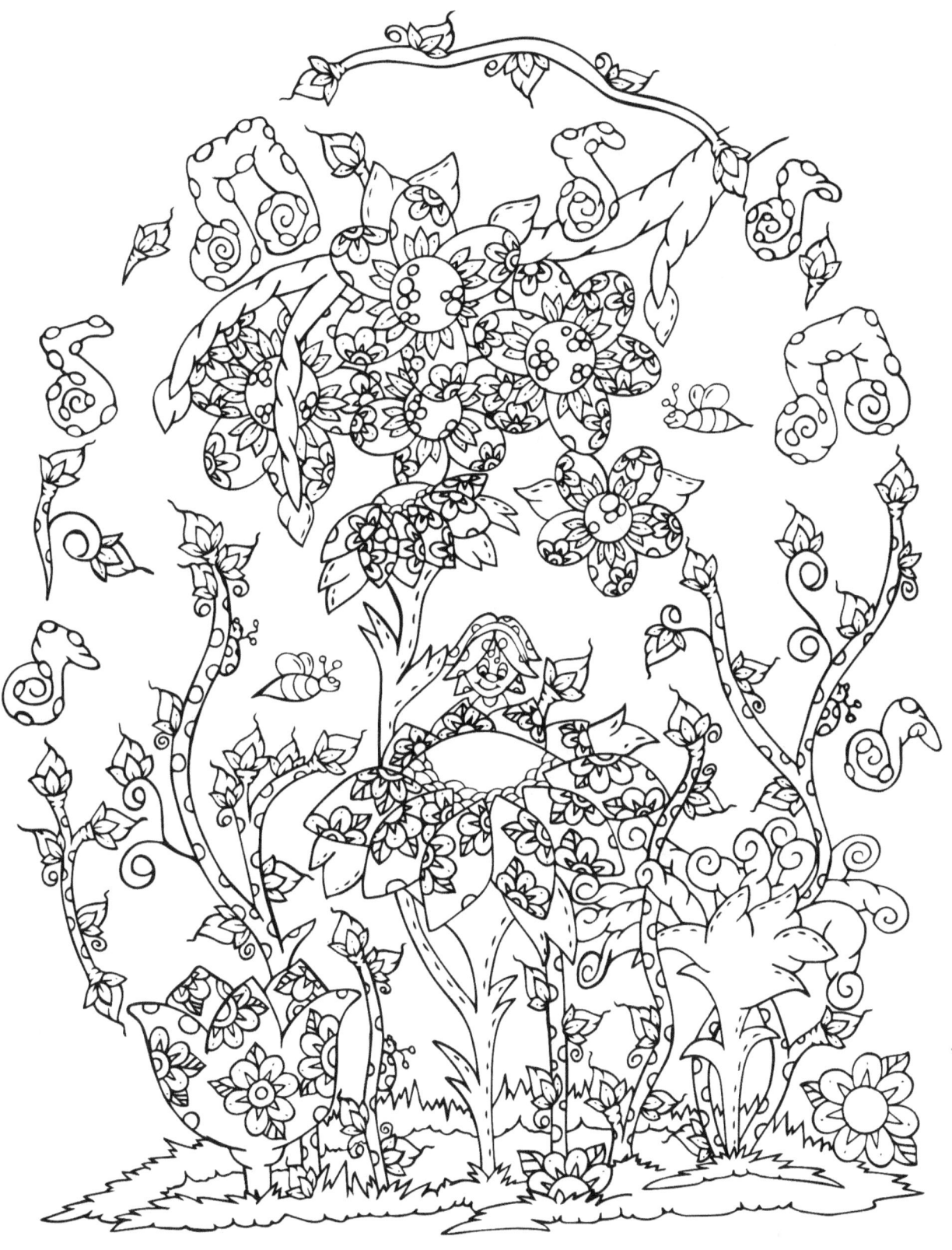

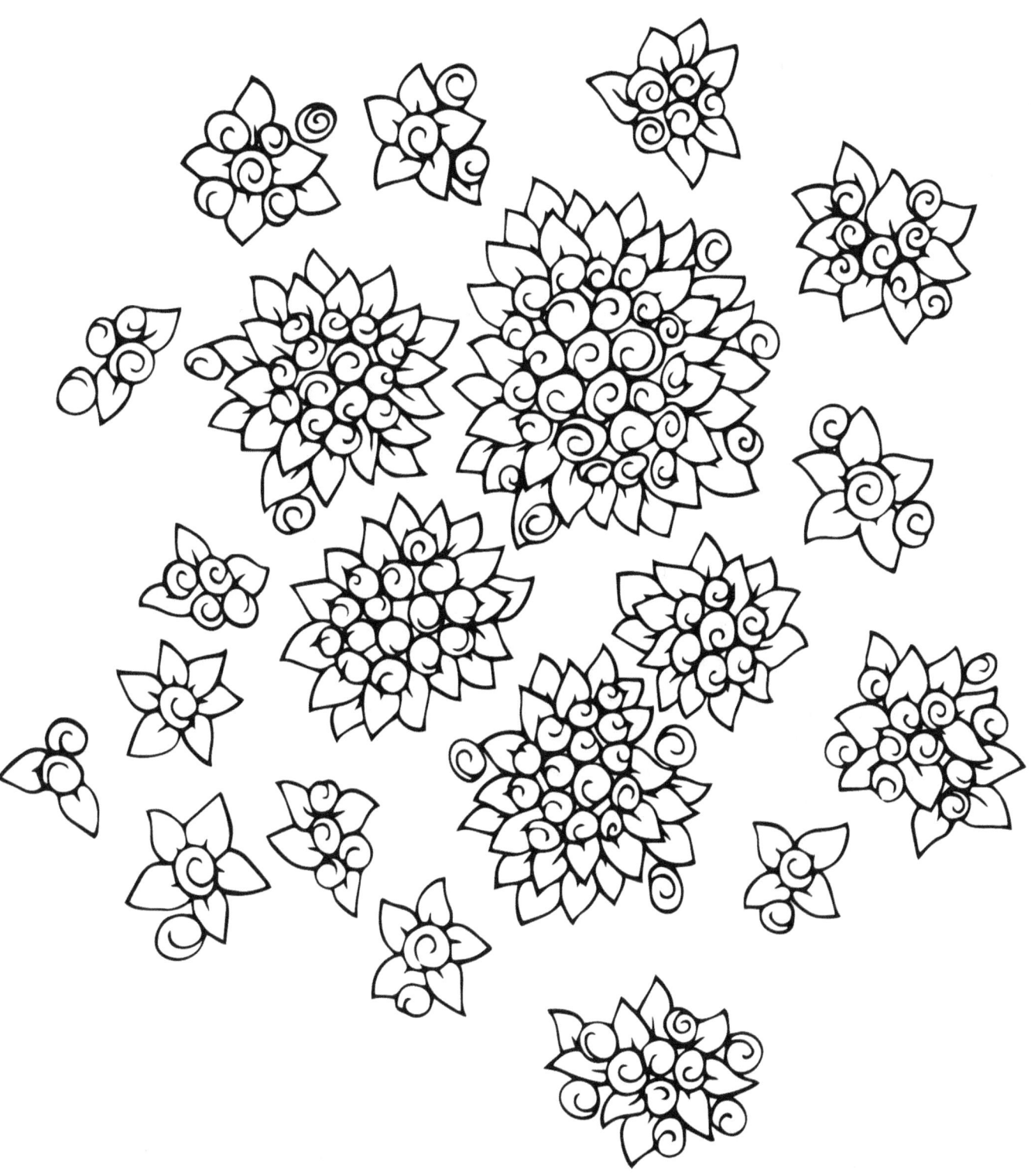

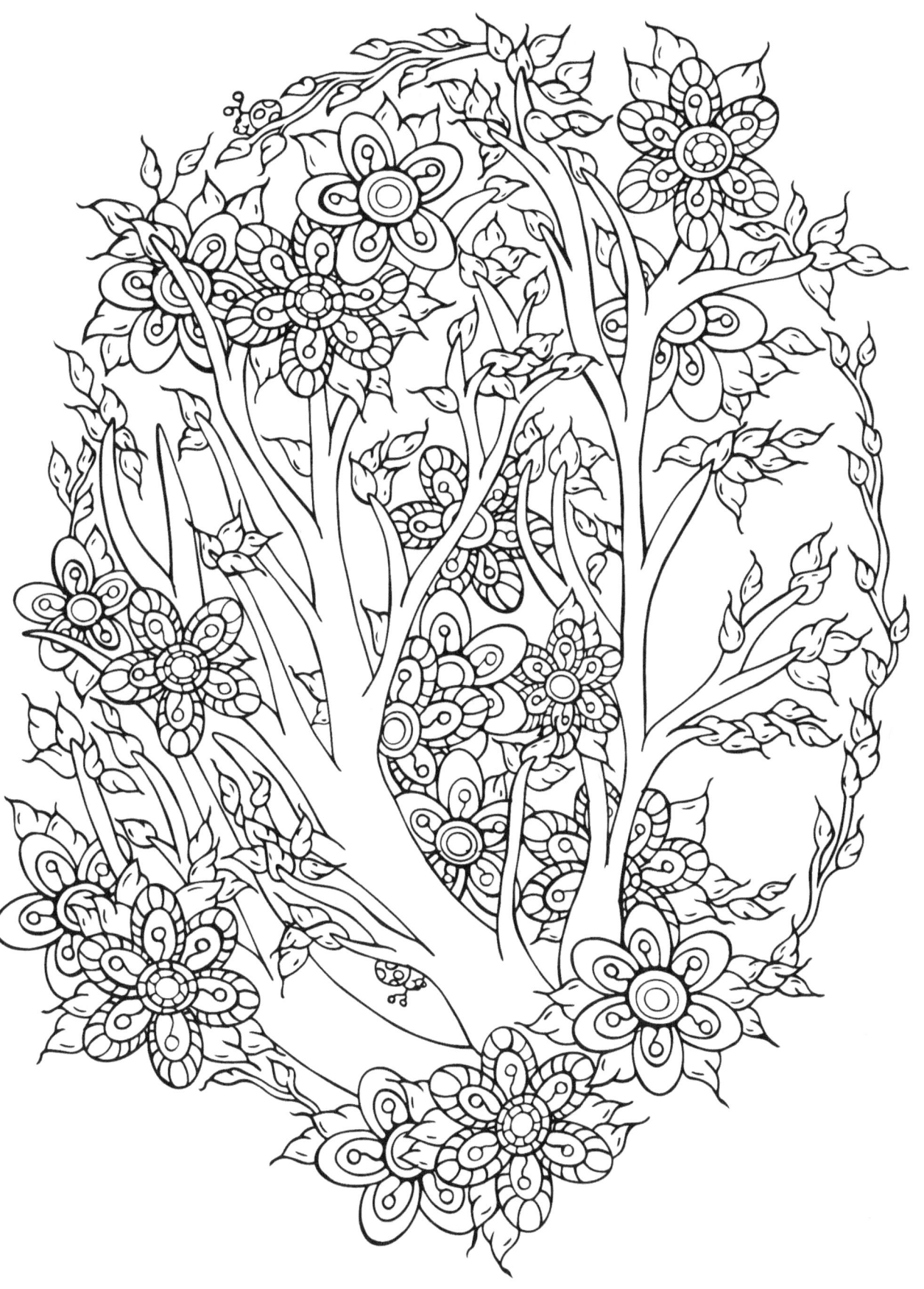

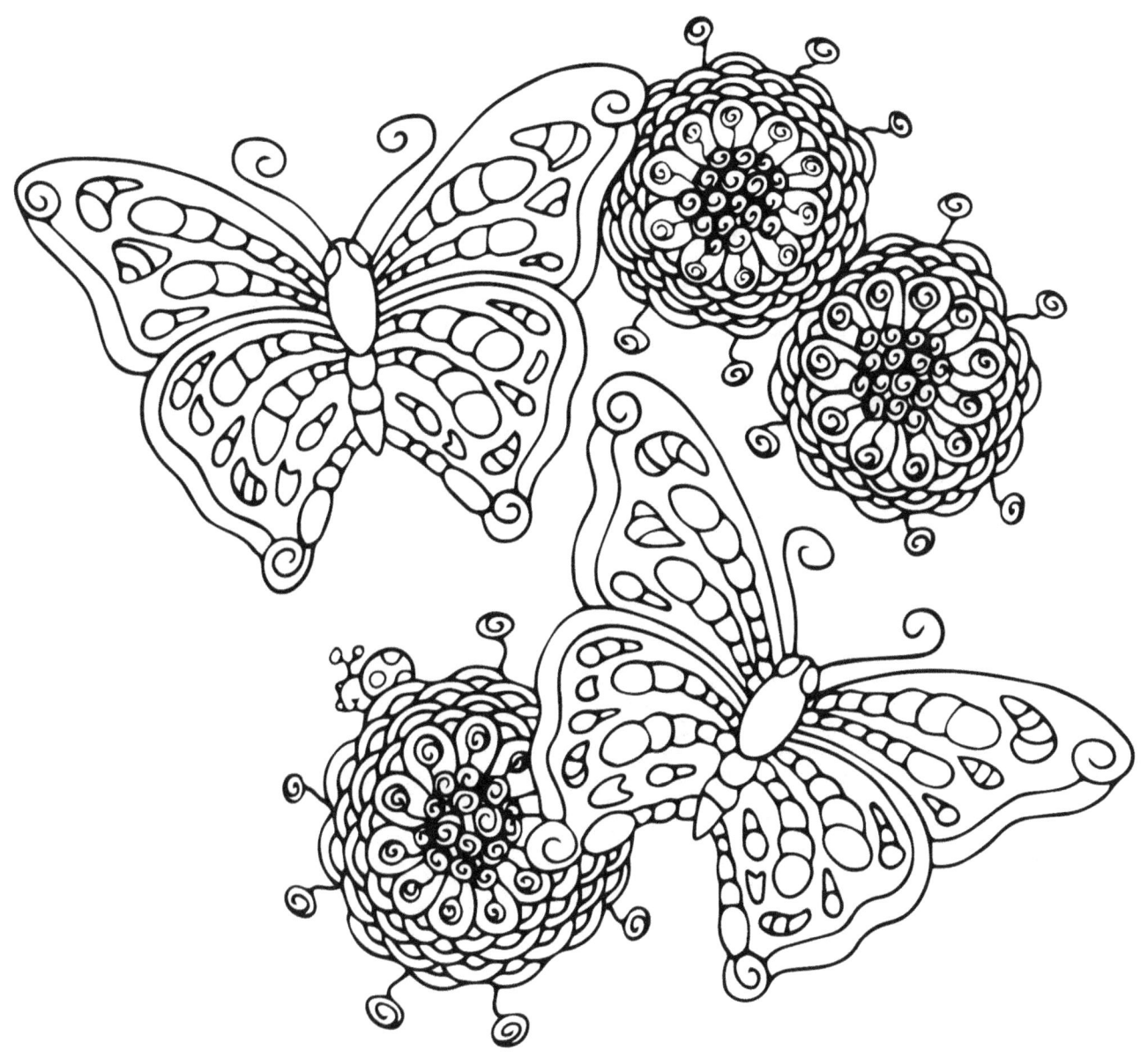

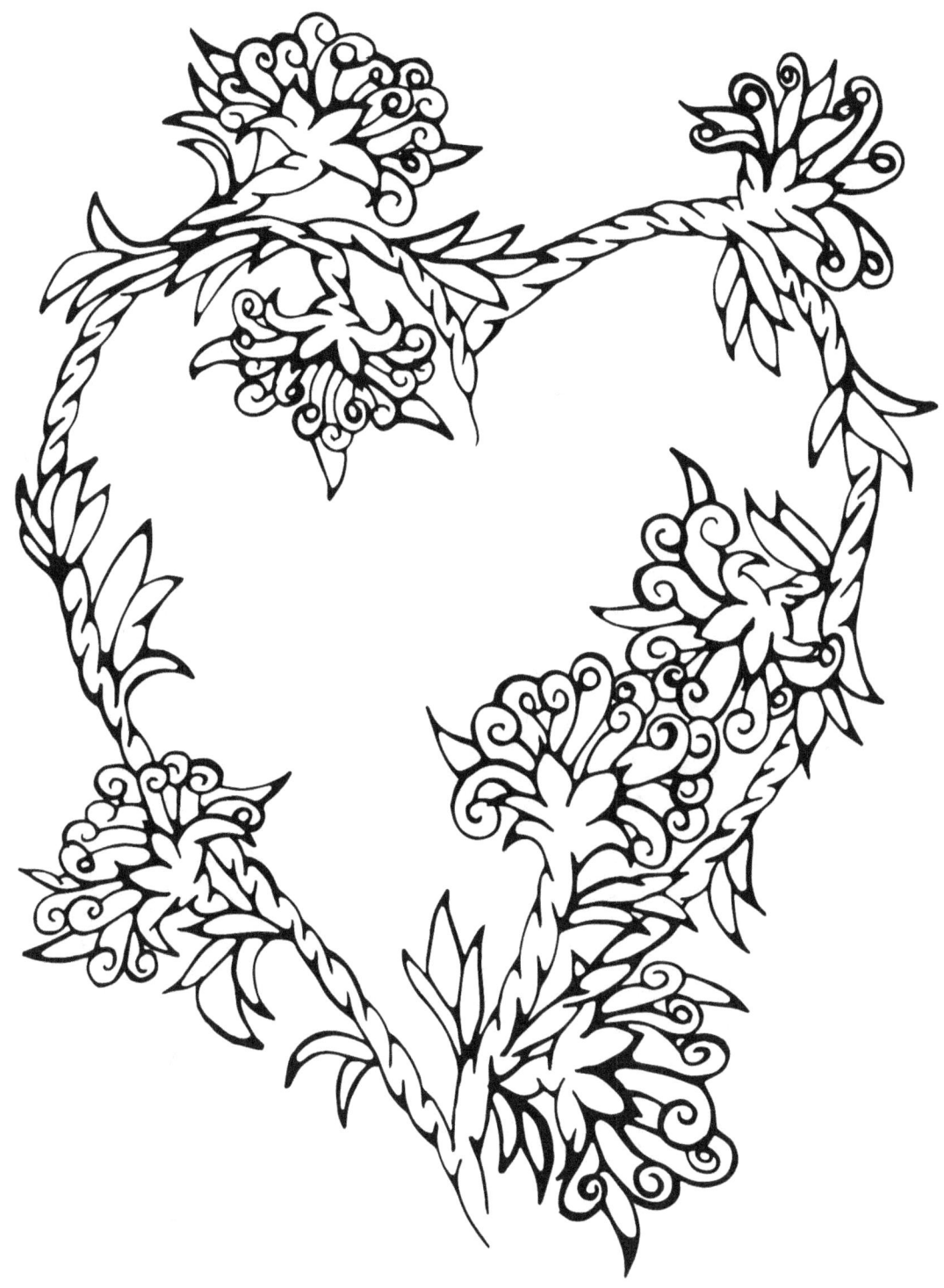

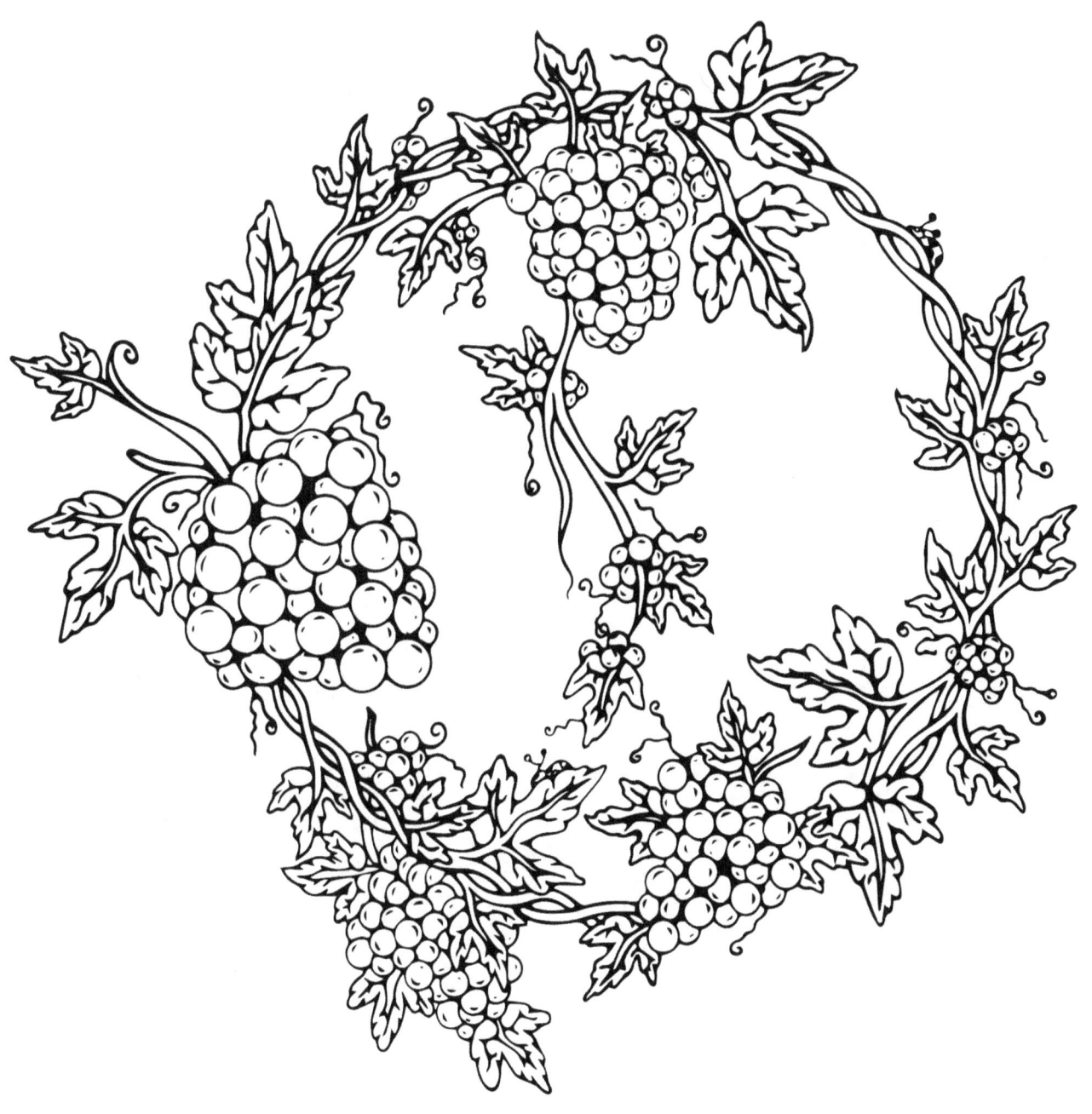

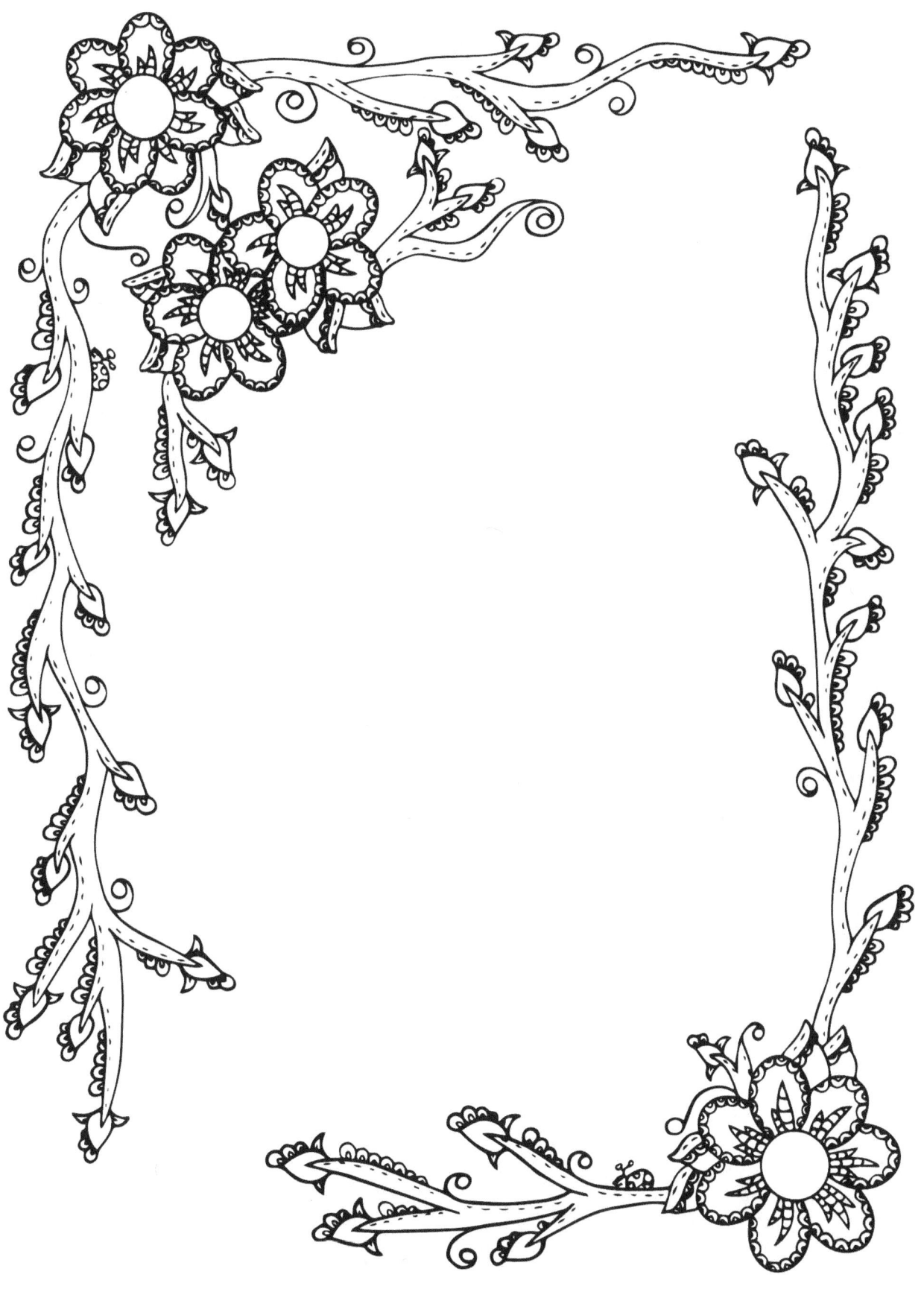

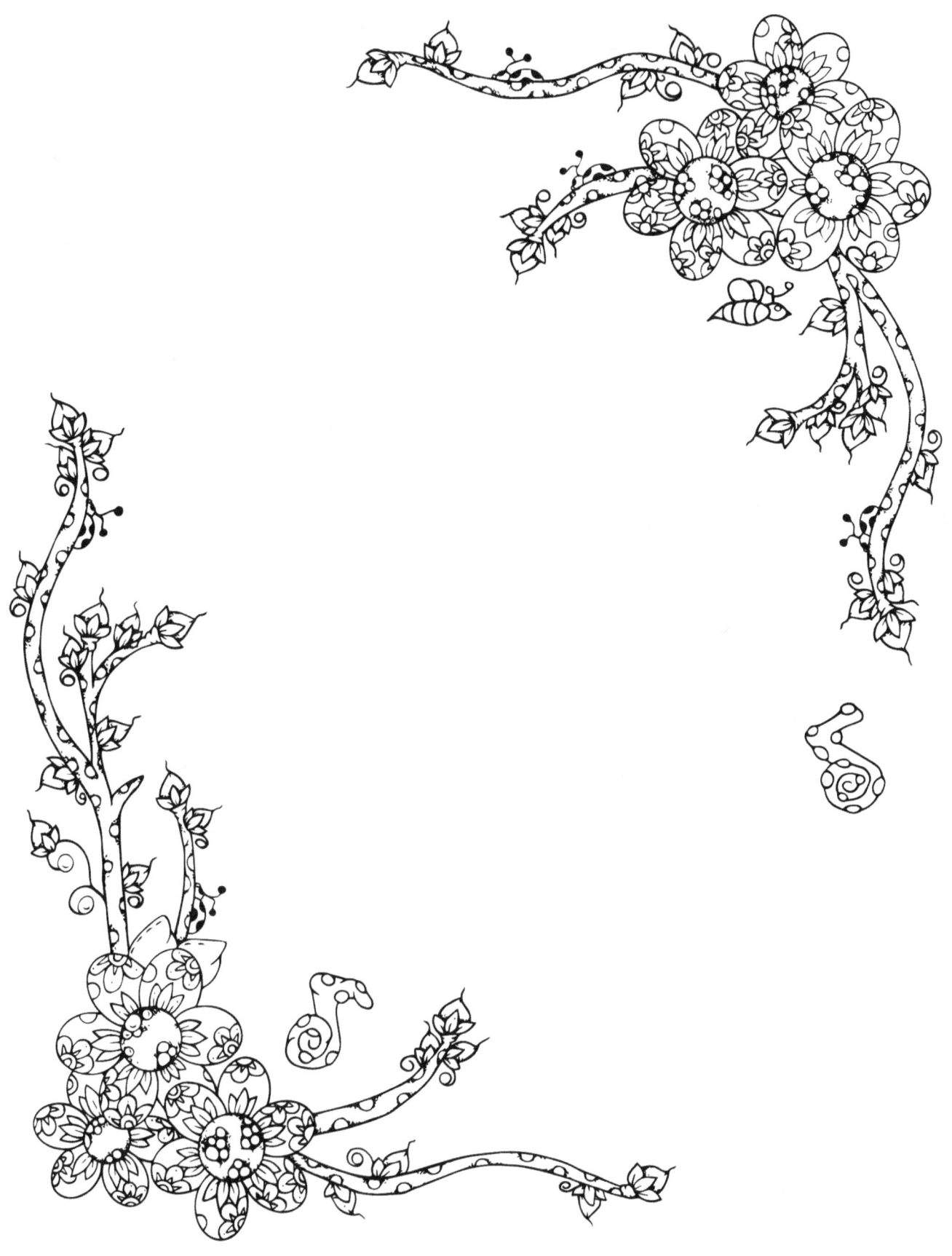

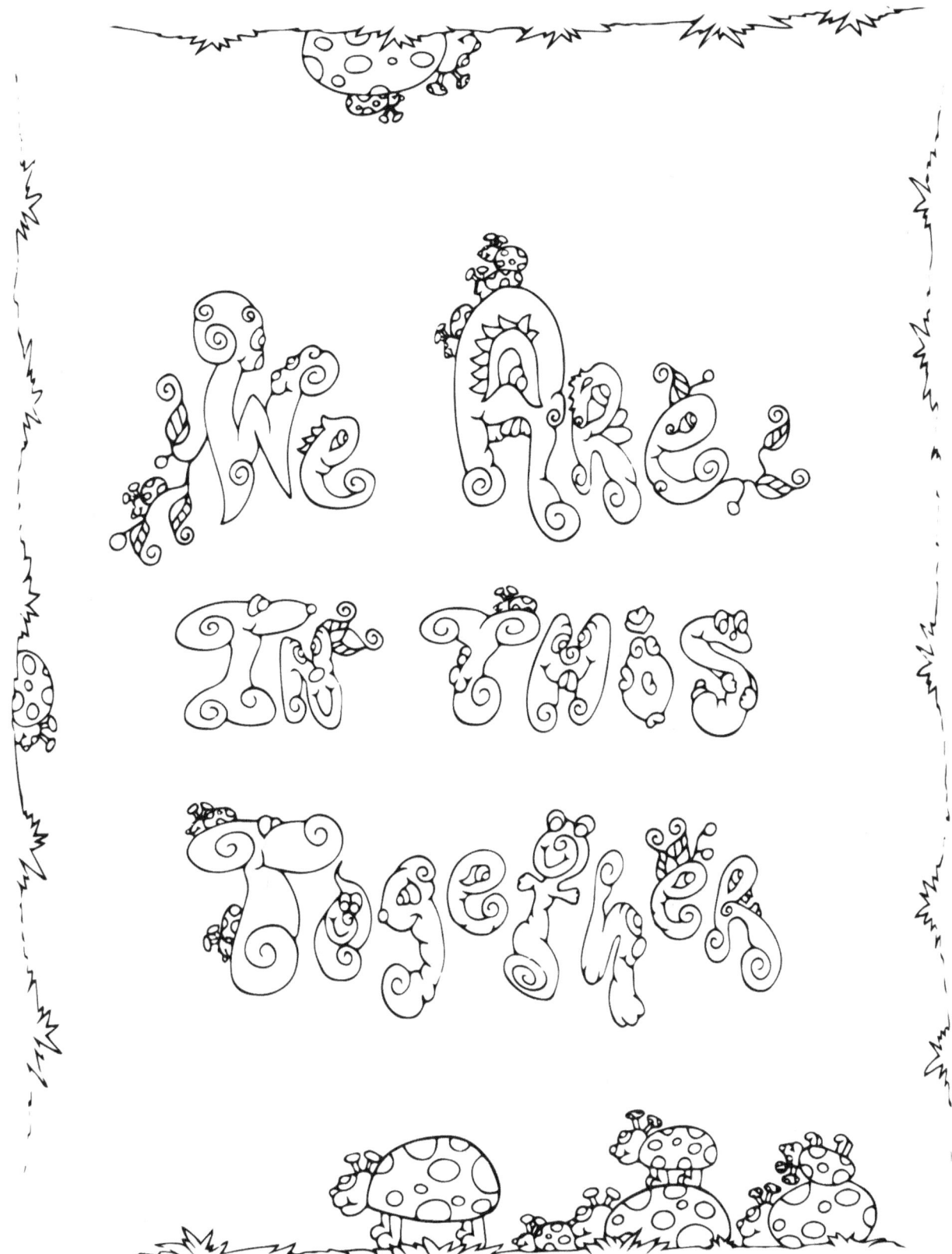

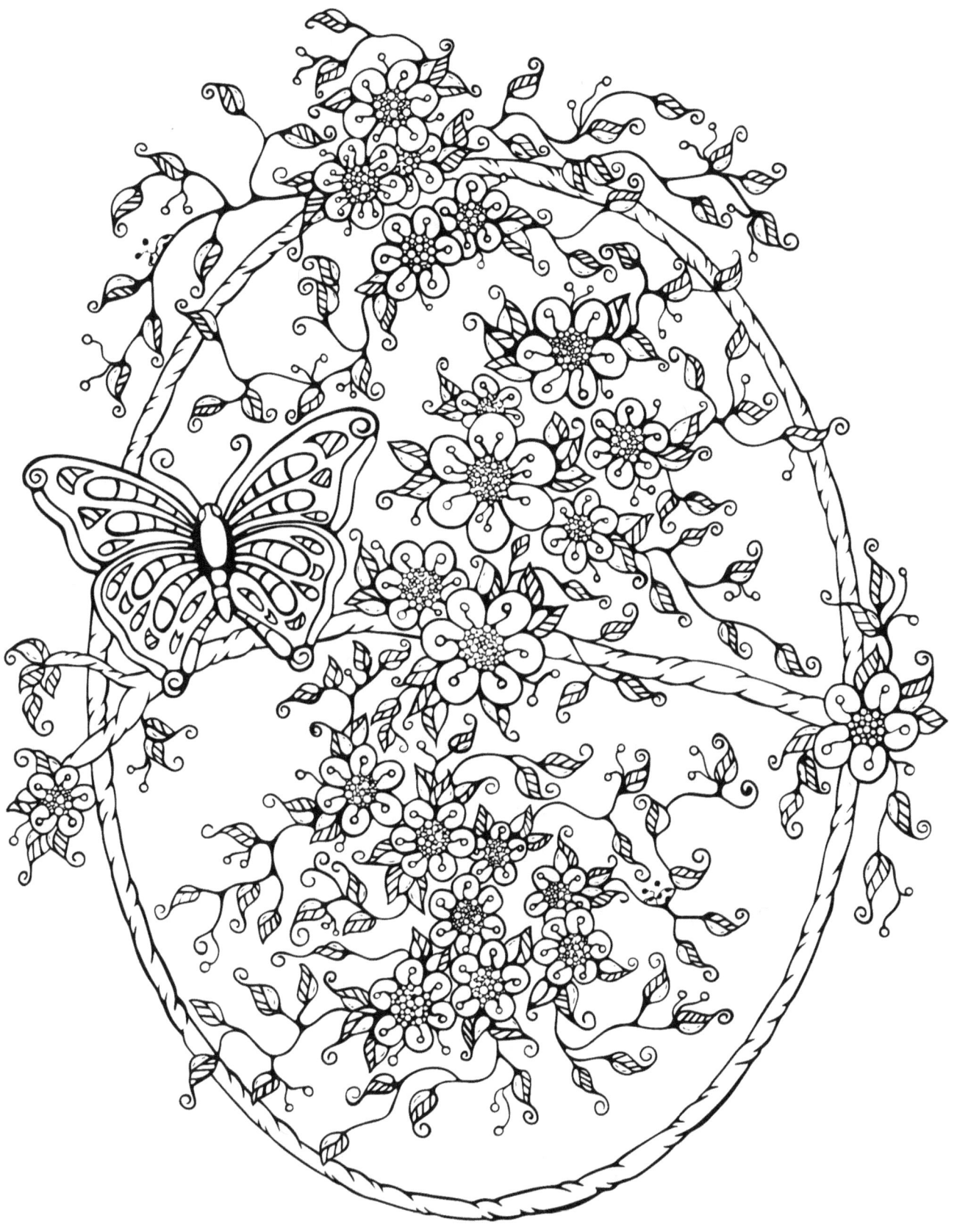

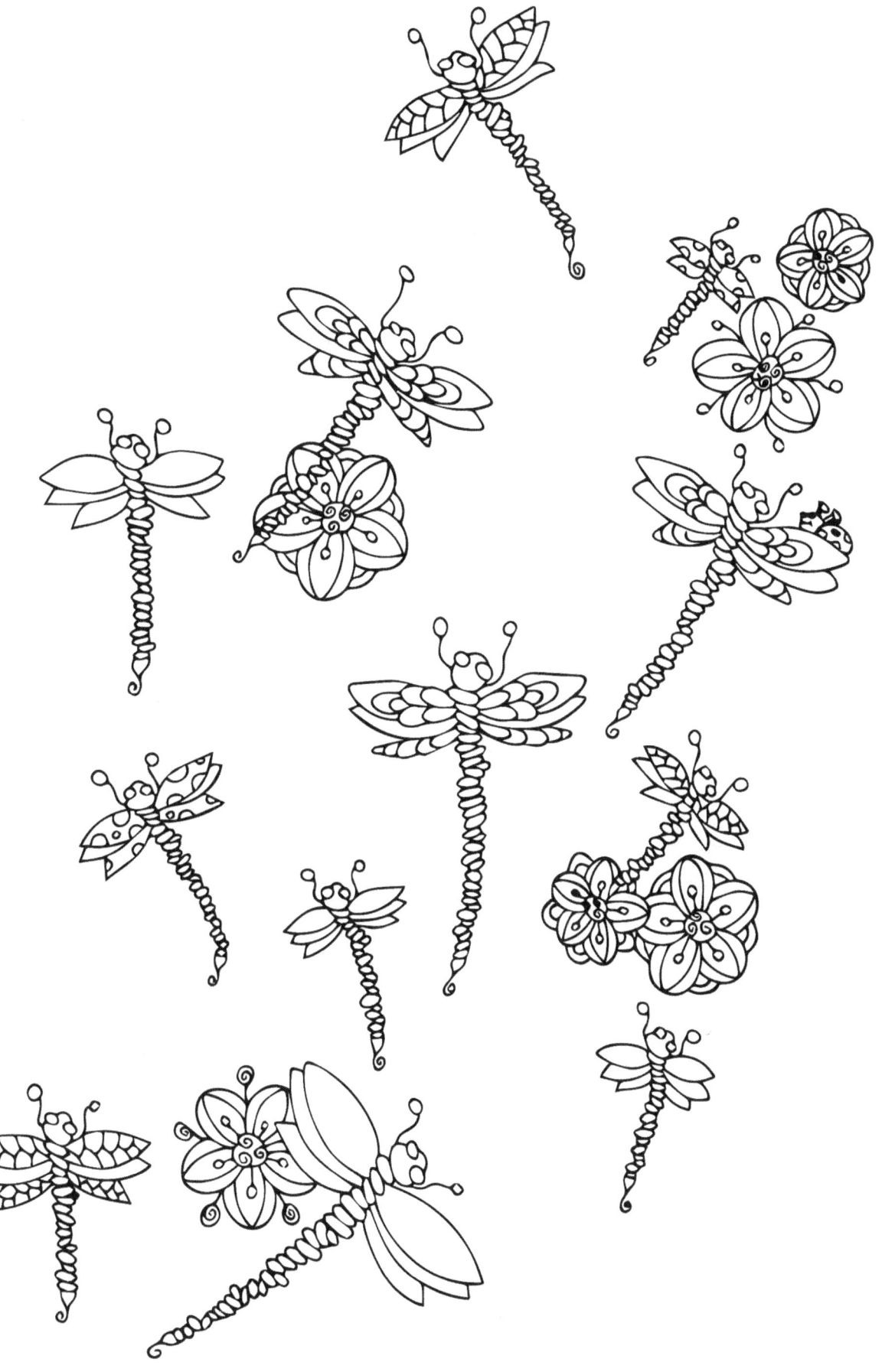

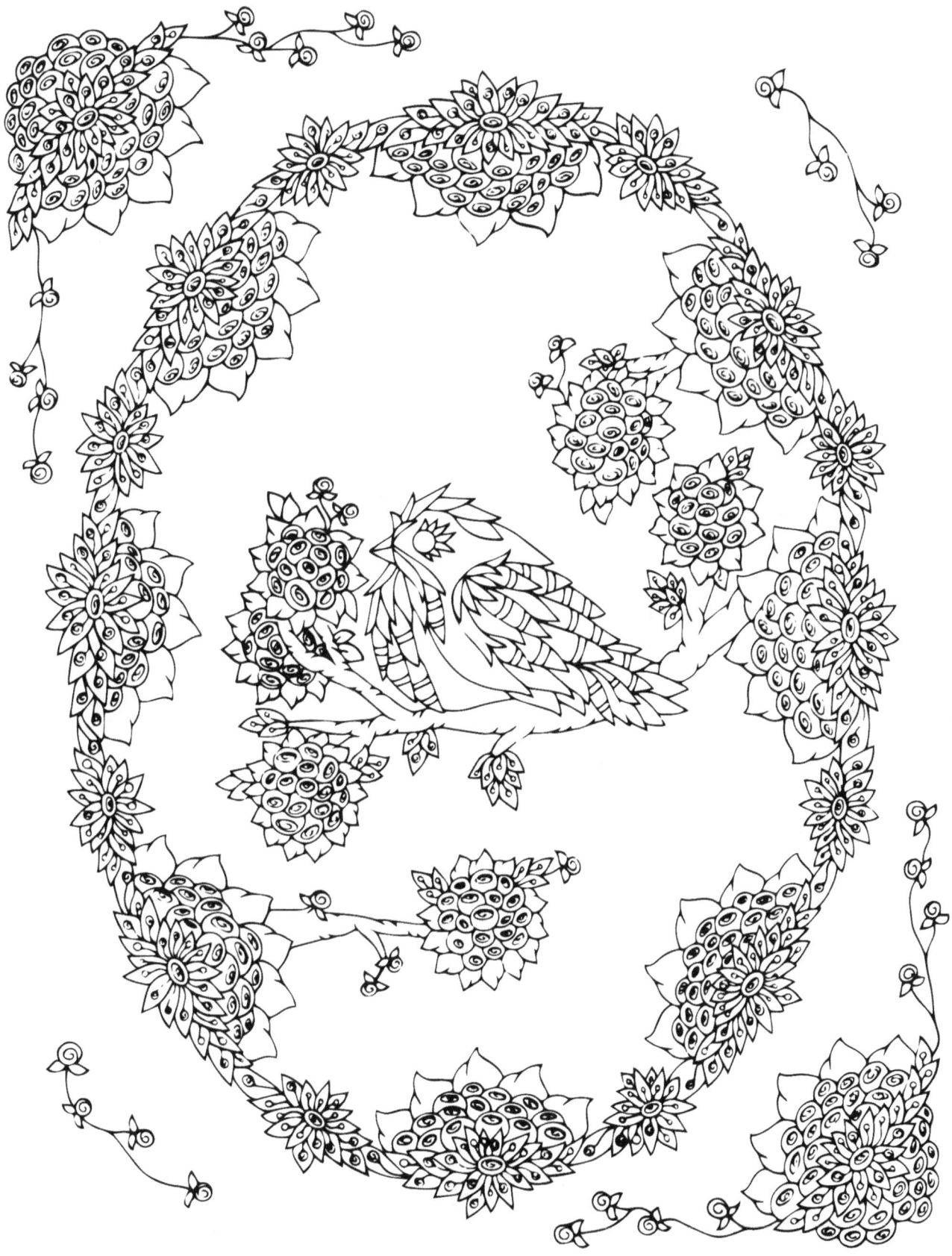

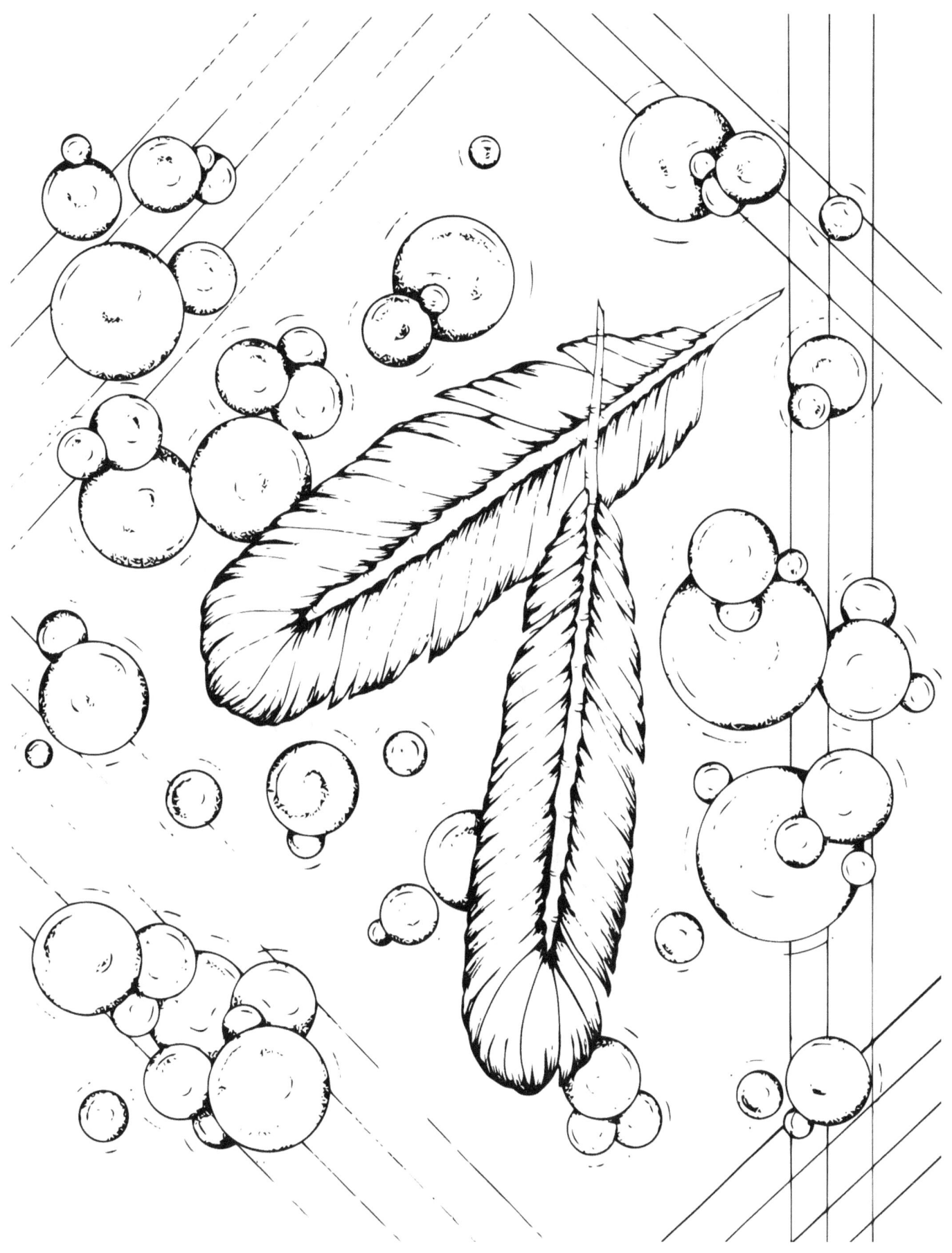

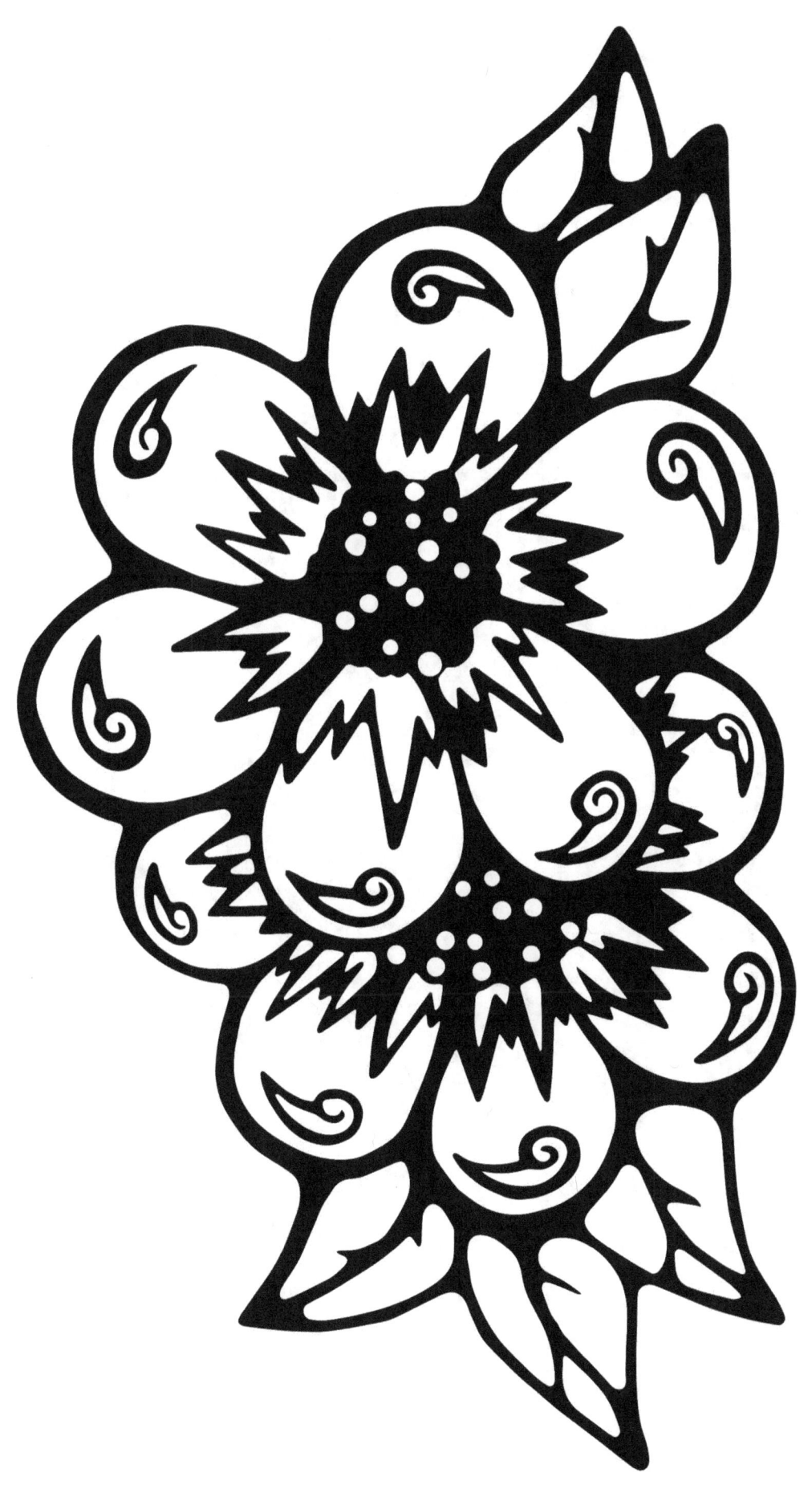

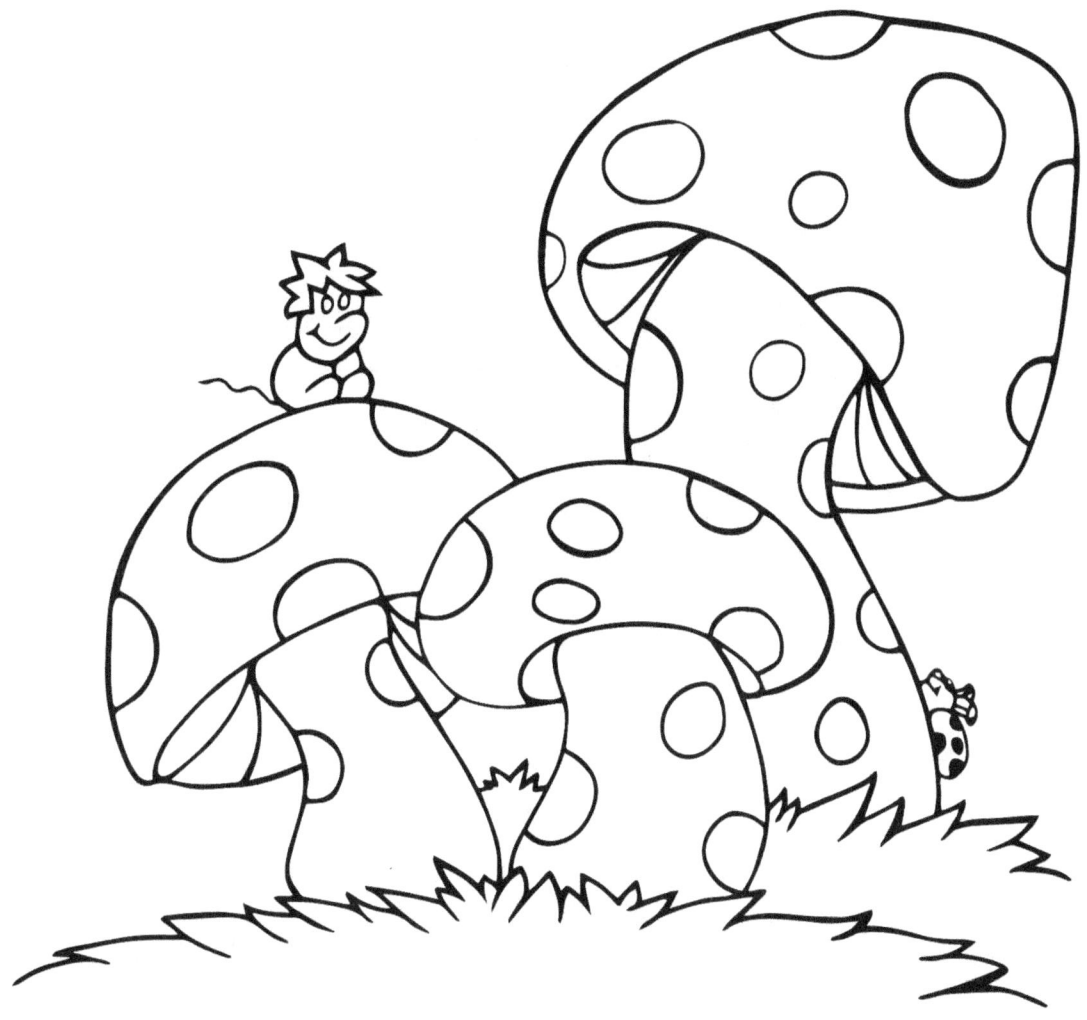

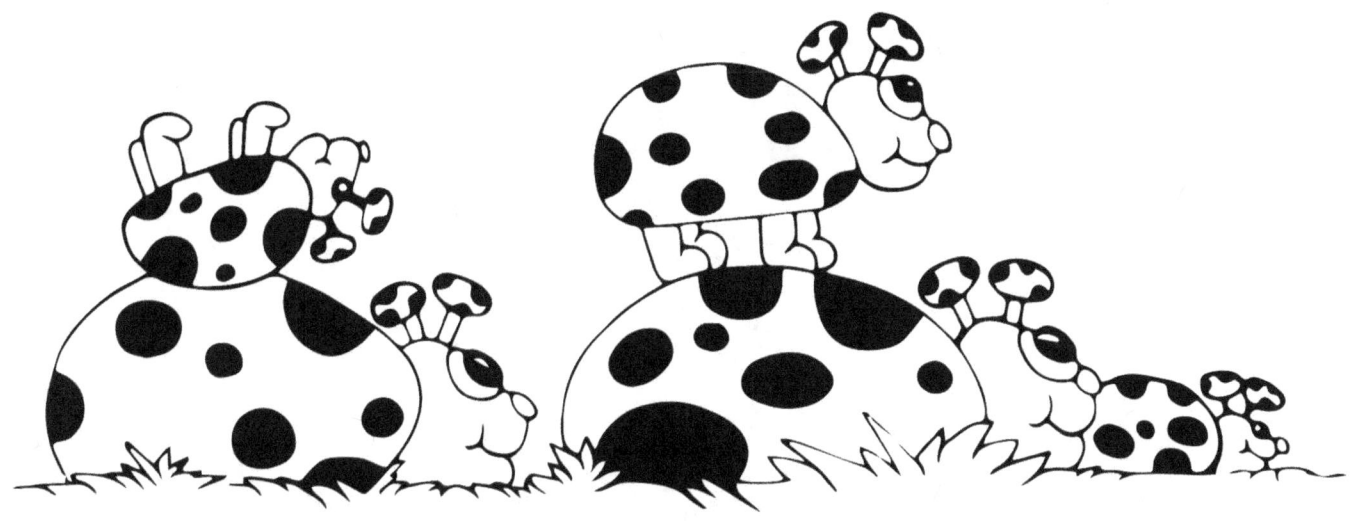

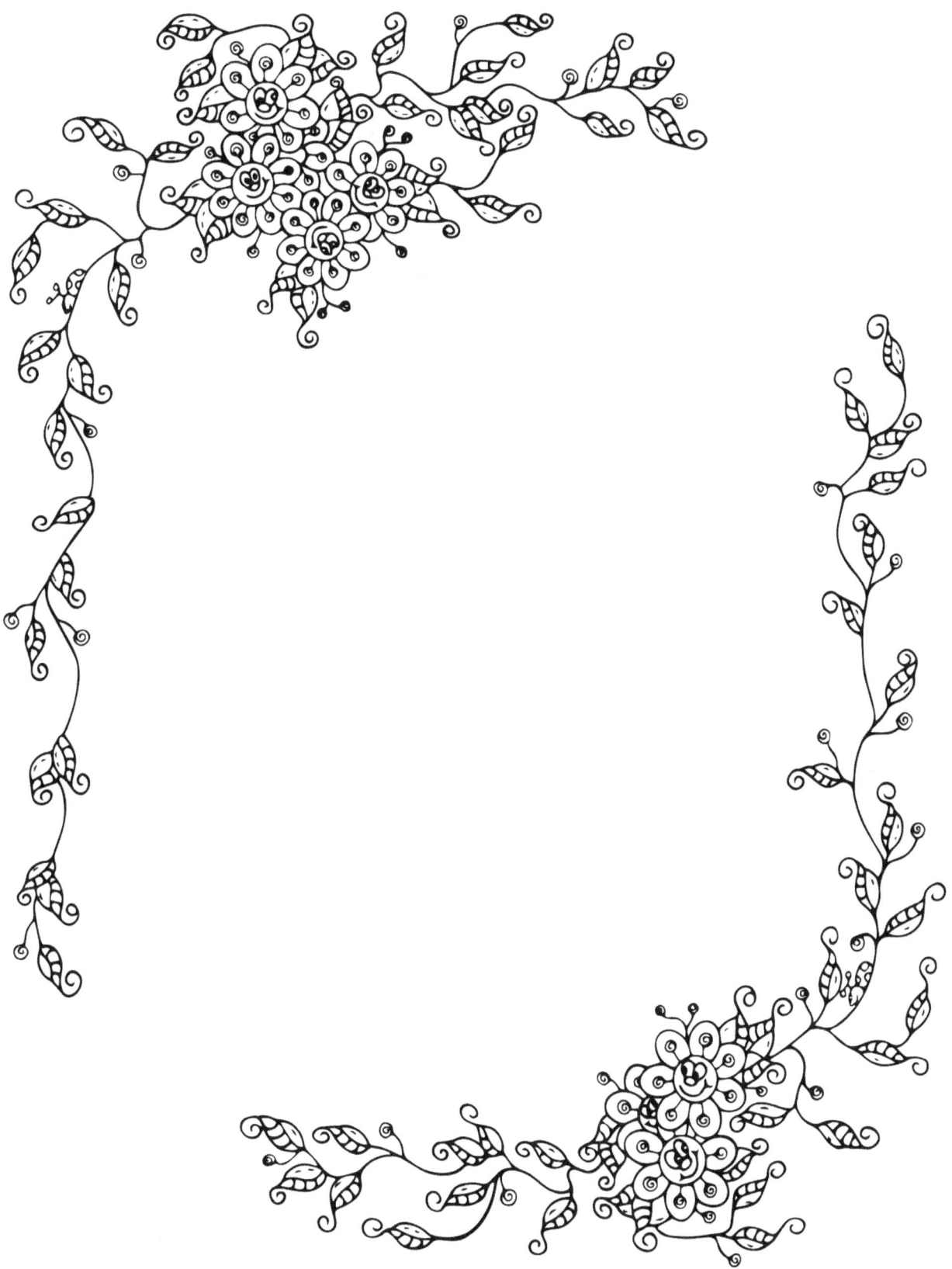

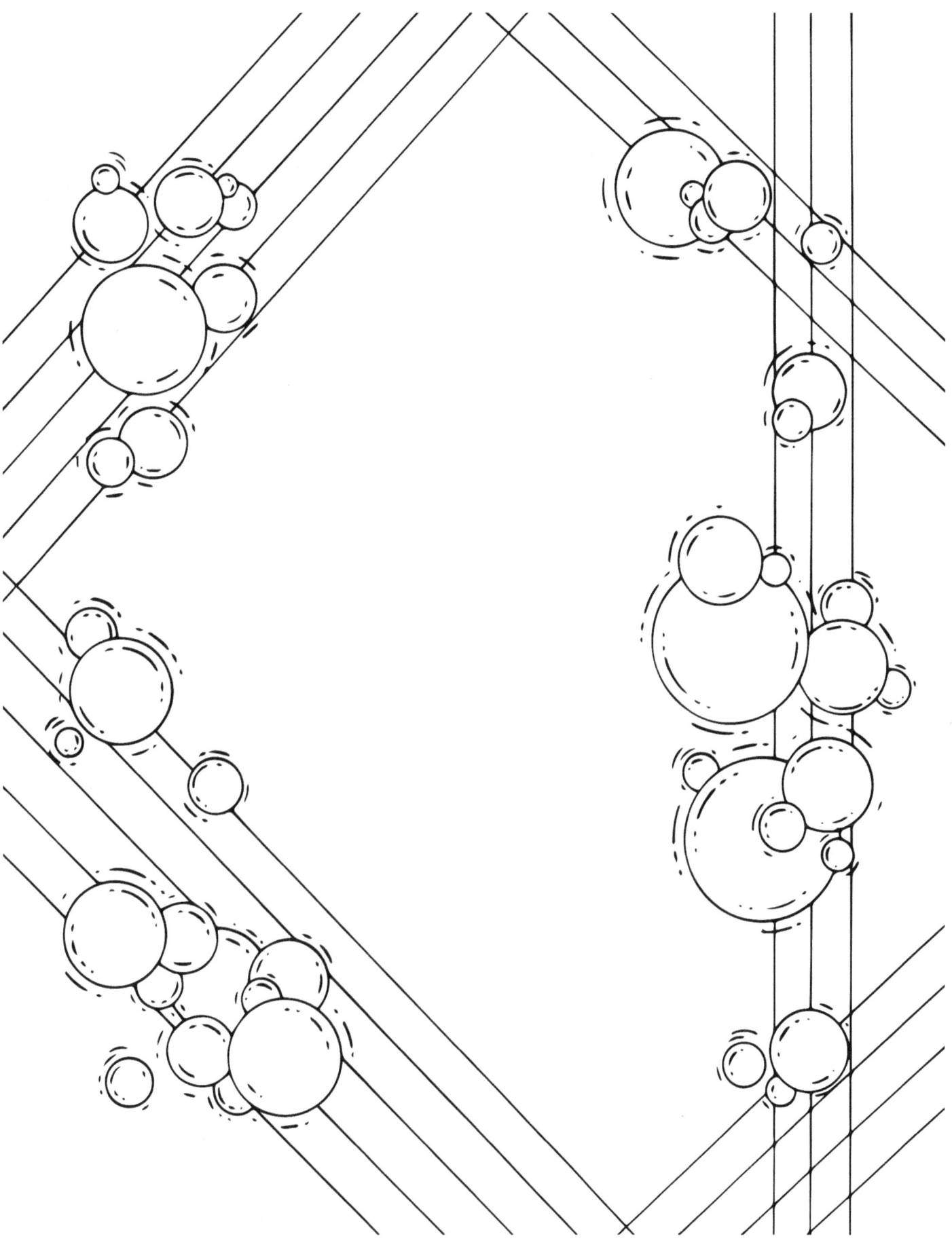

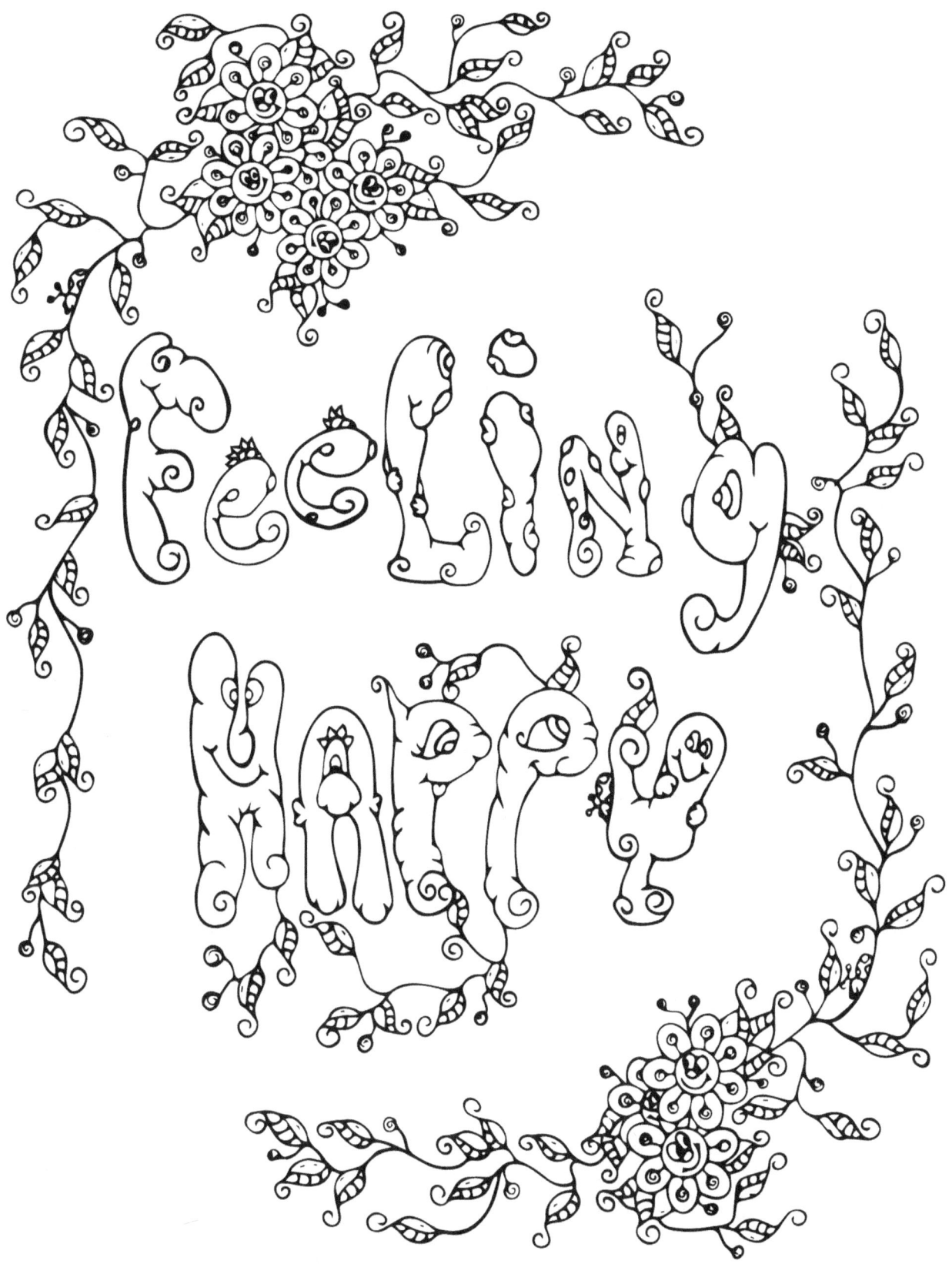

Feeling Happy

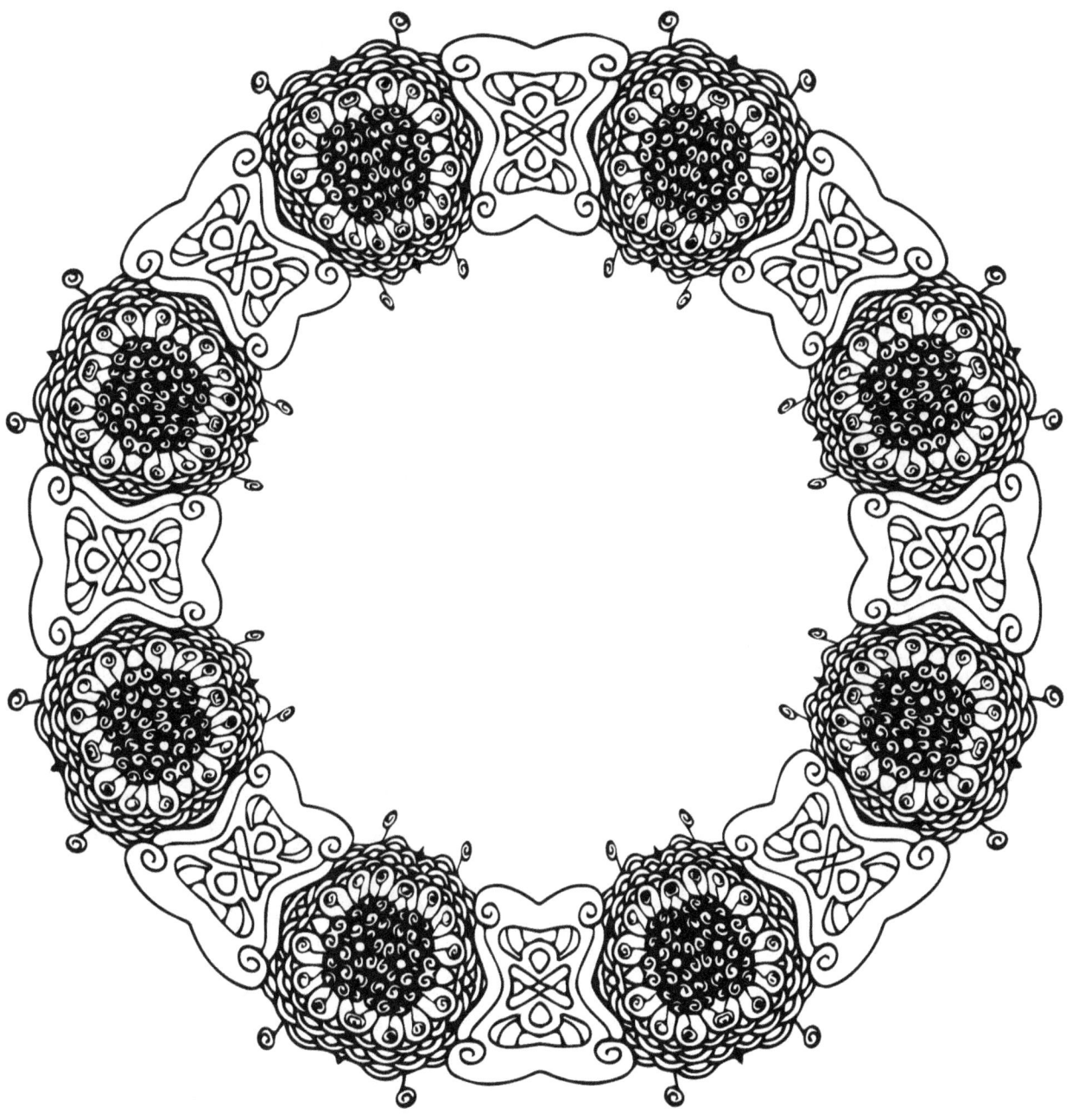

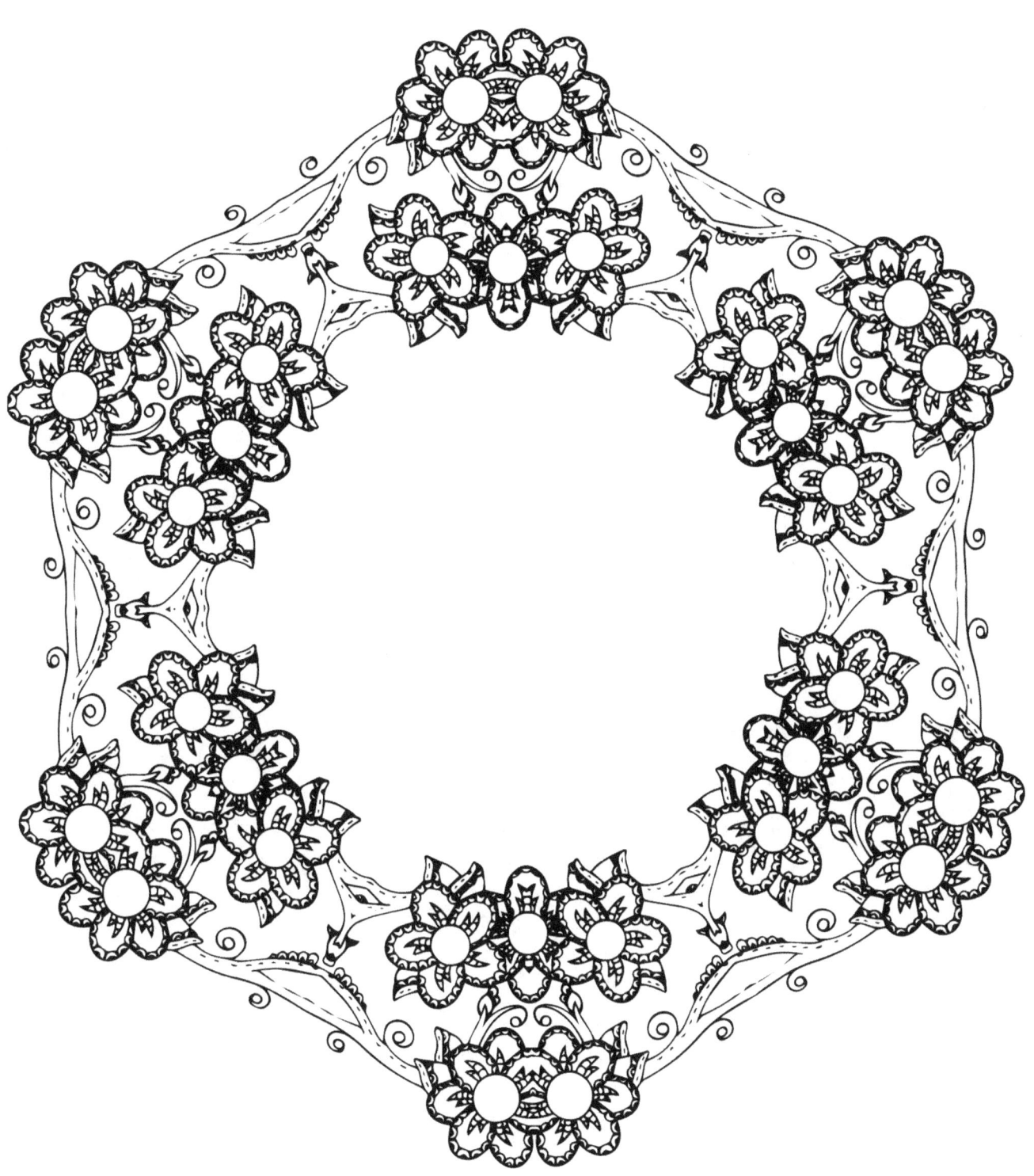

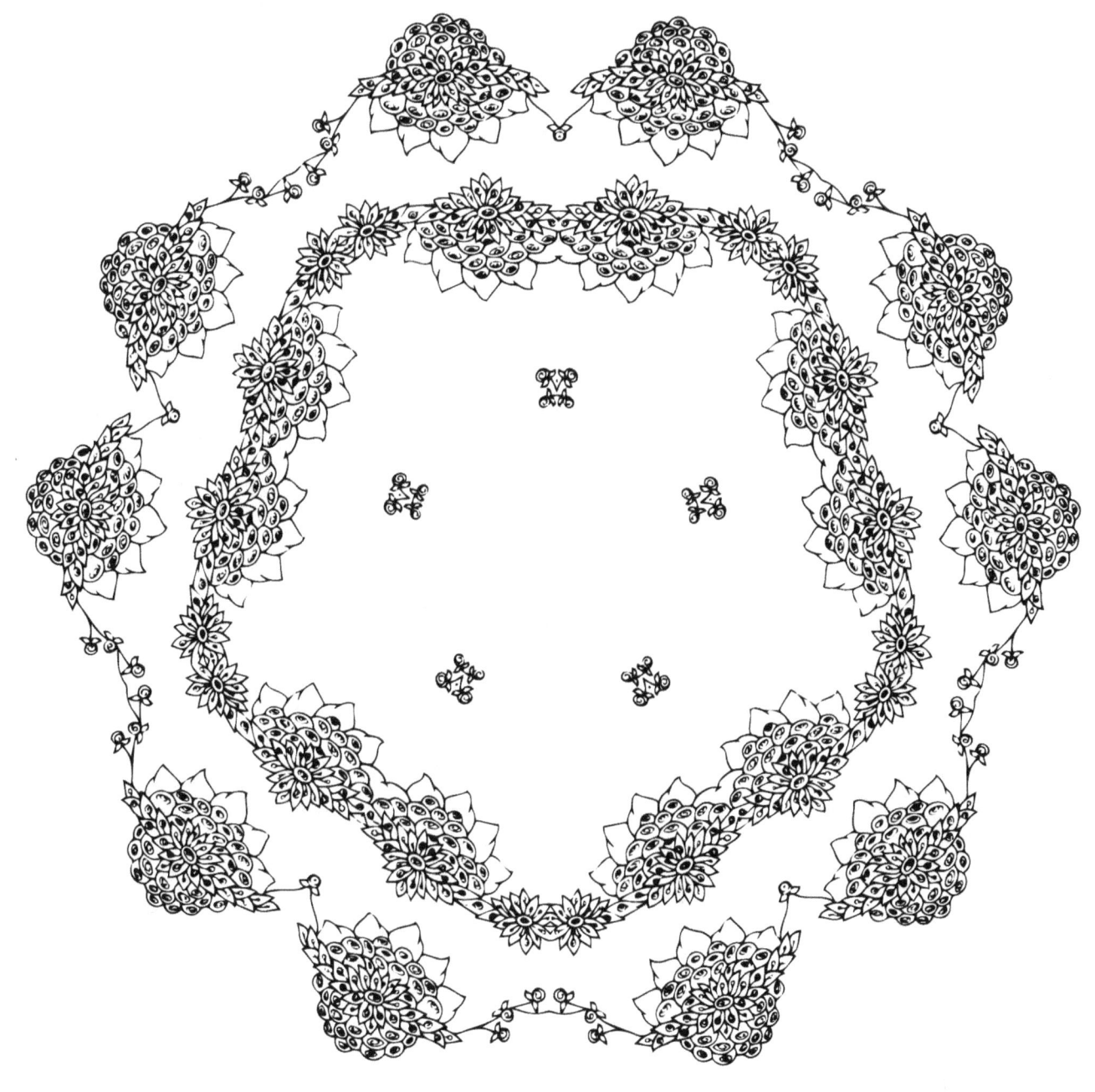

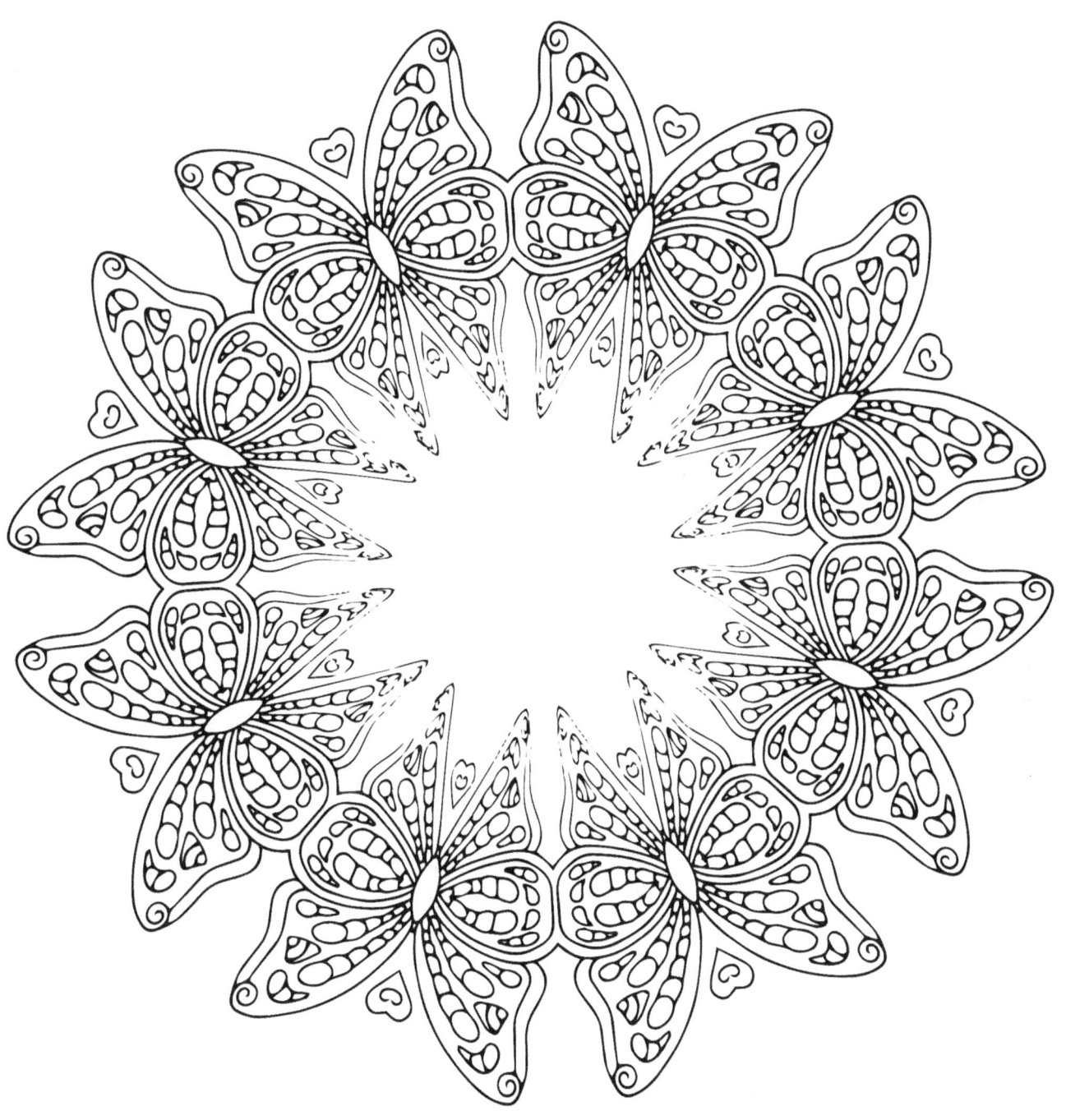

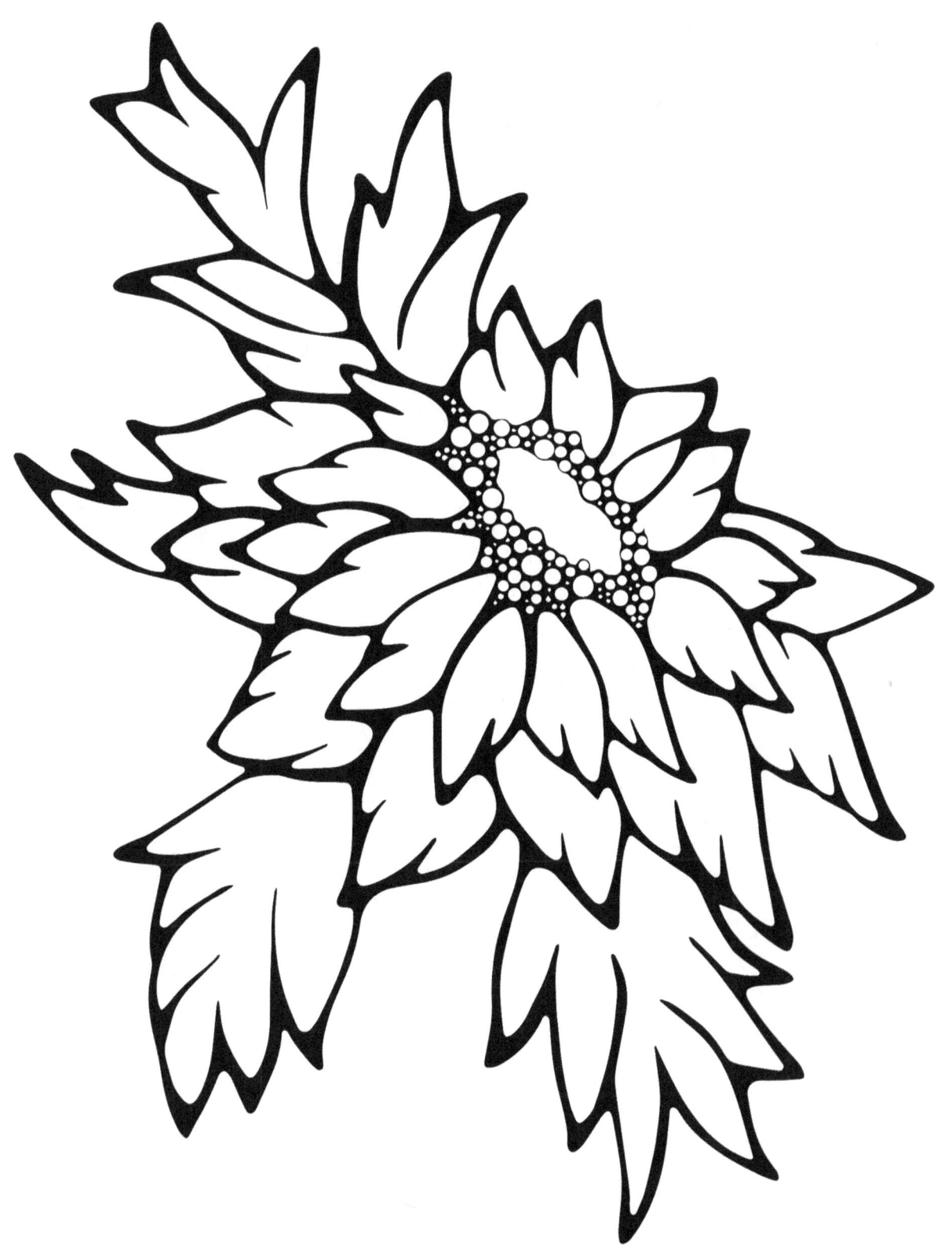

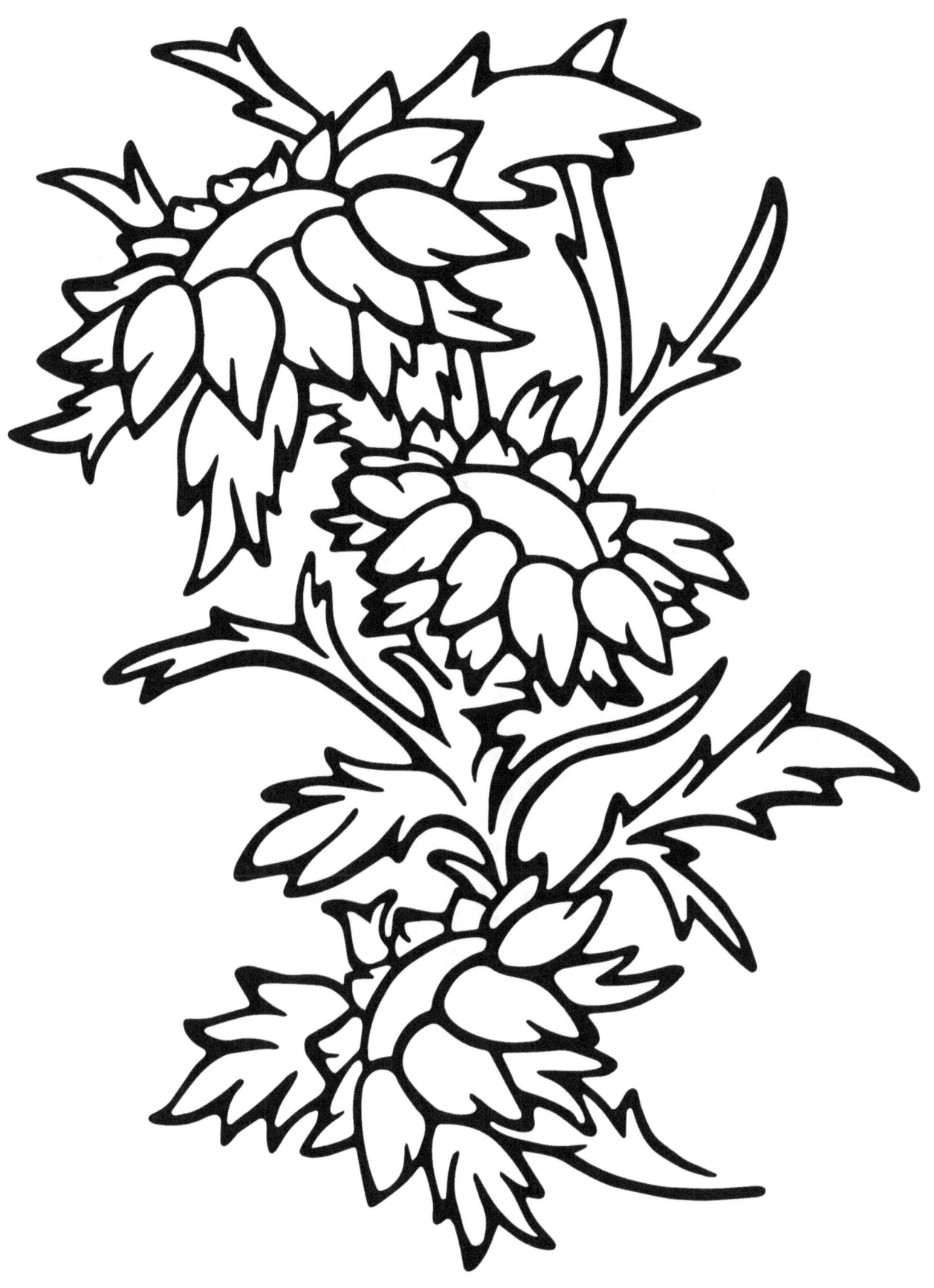

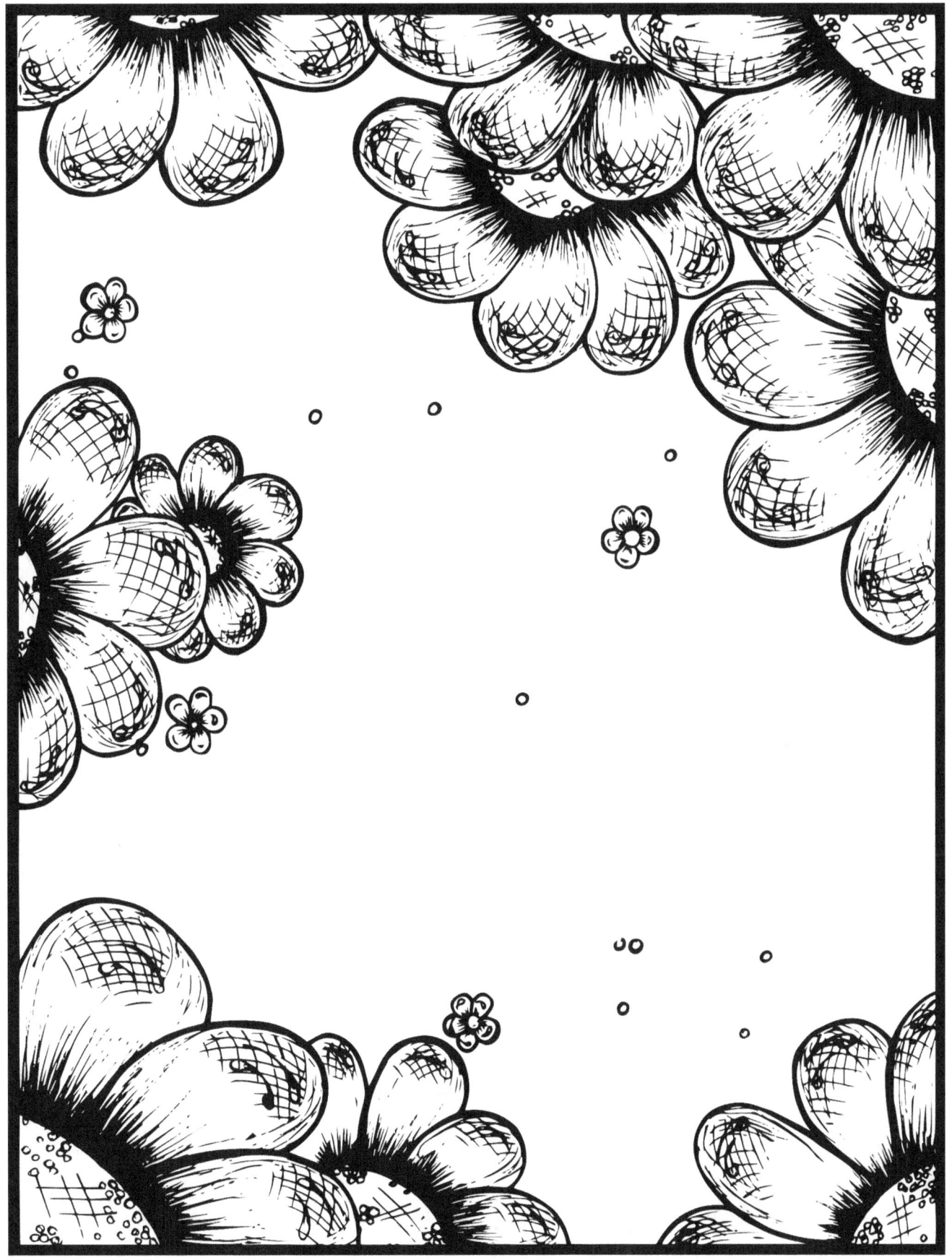

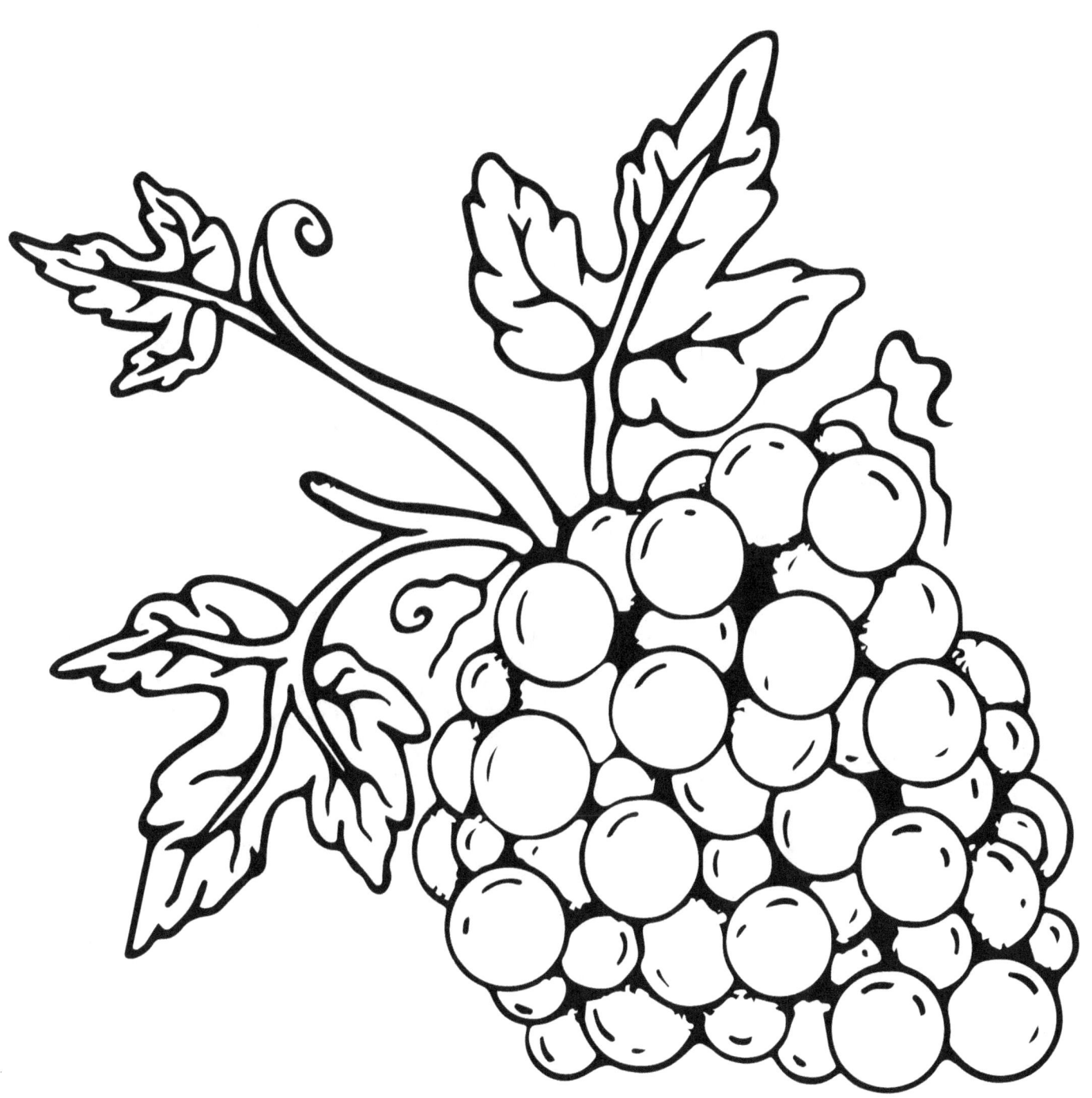

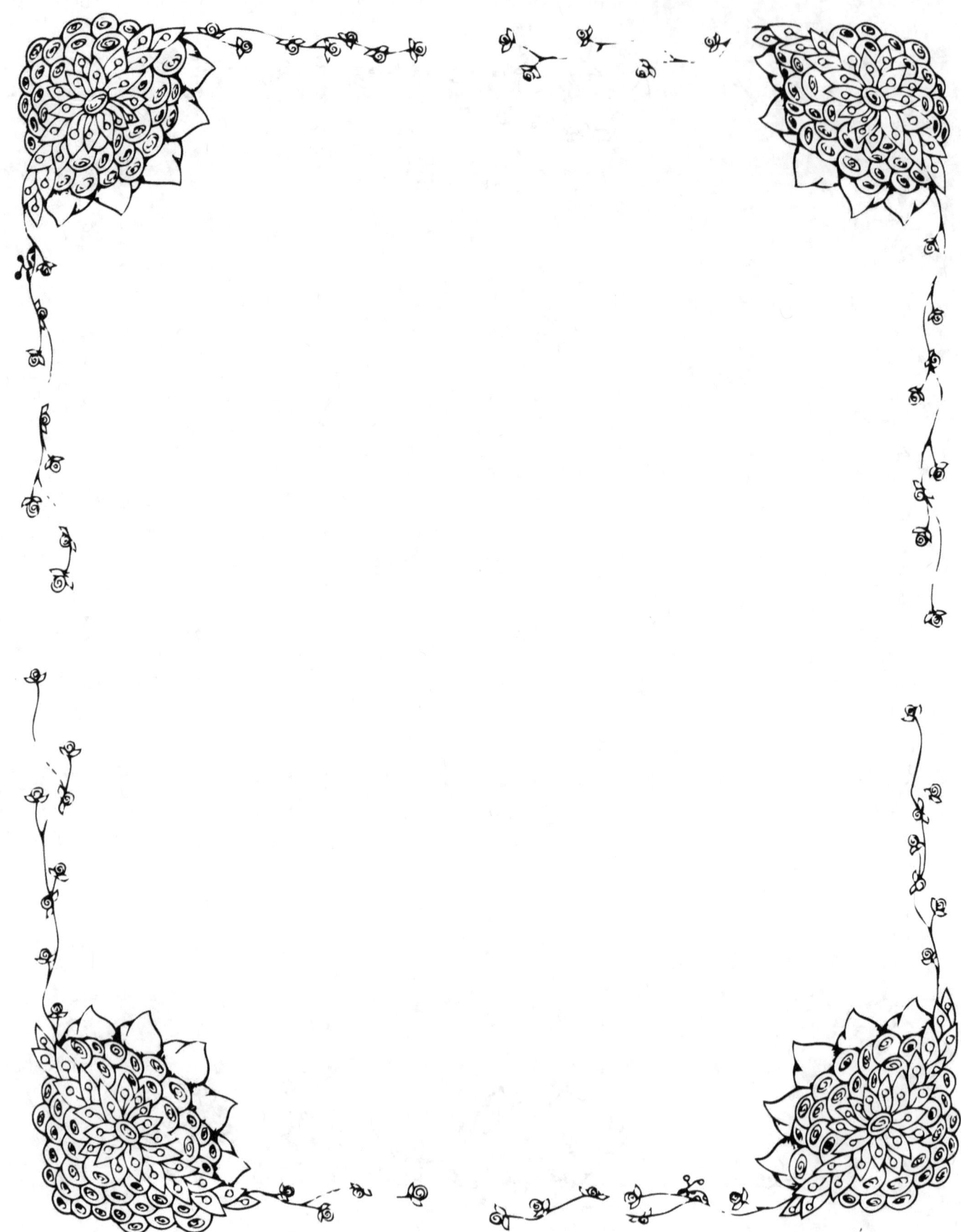

Bonnie S. MacLachlan ©

www.ArtZillustrations.com

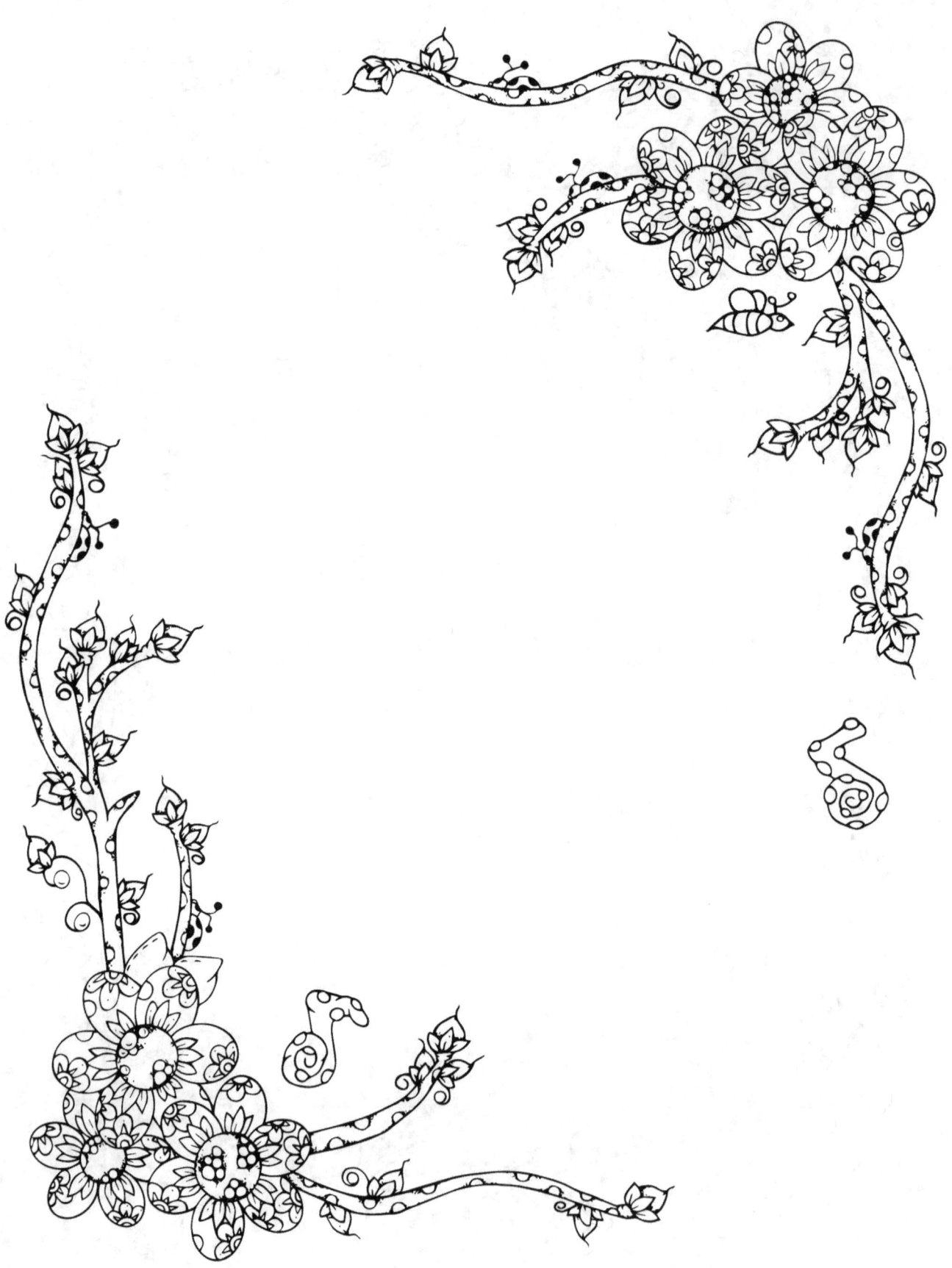

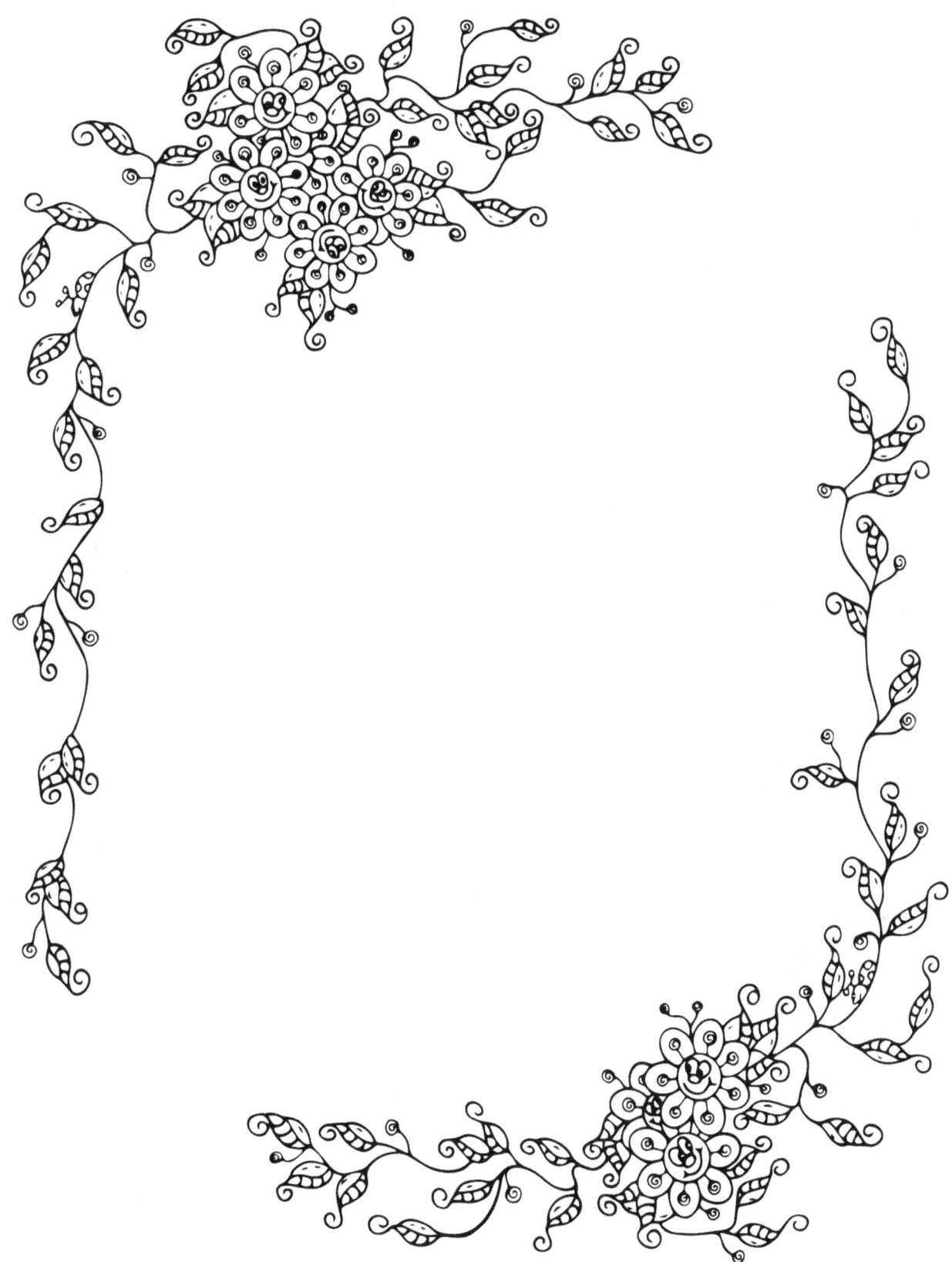

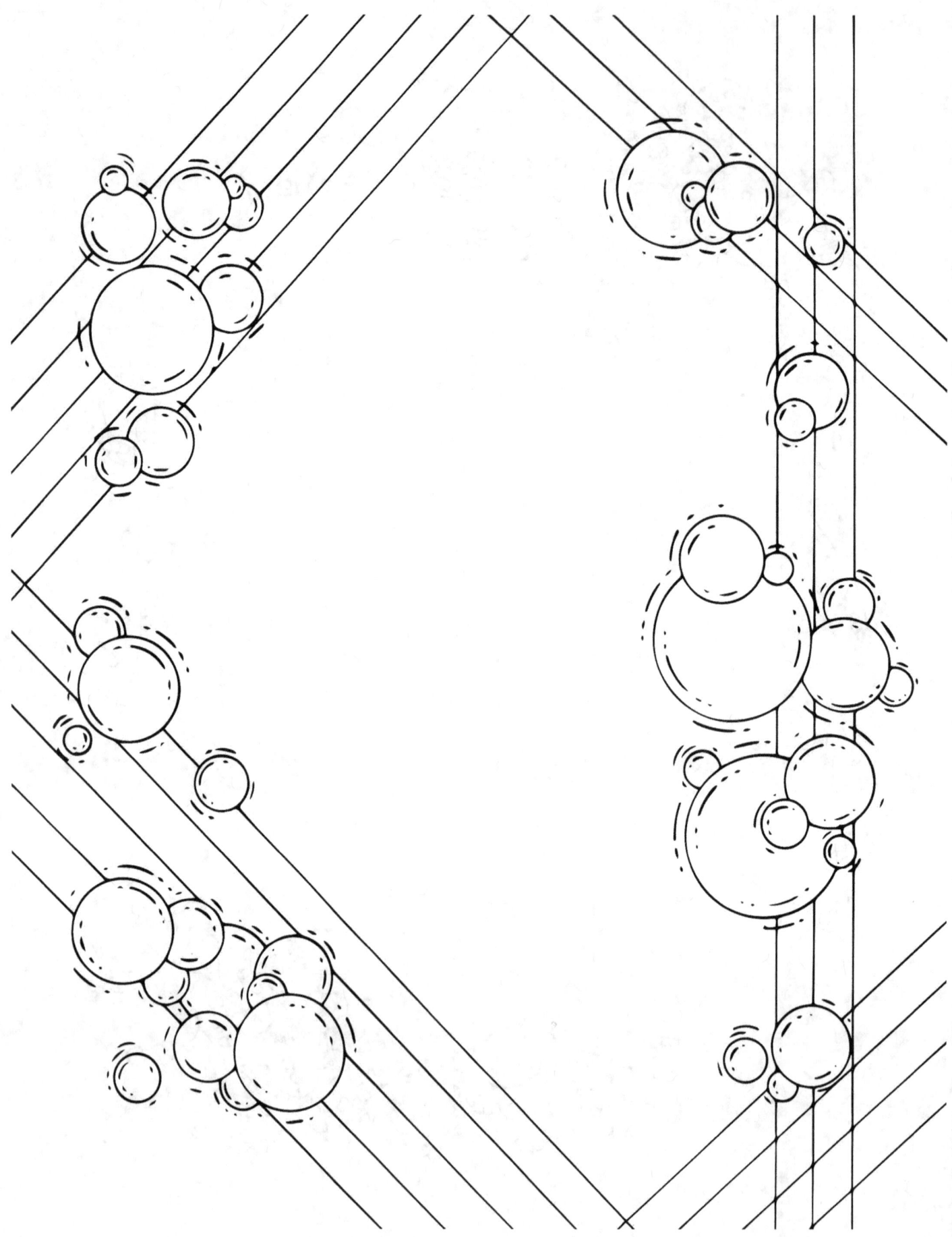

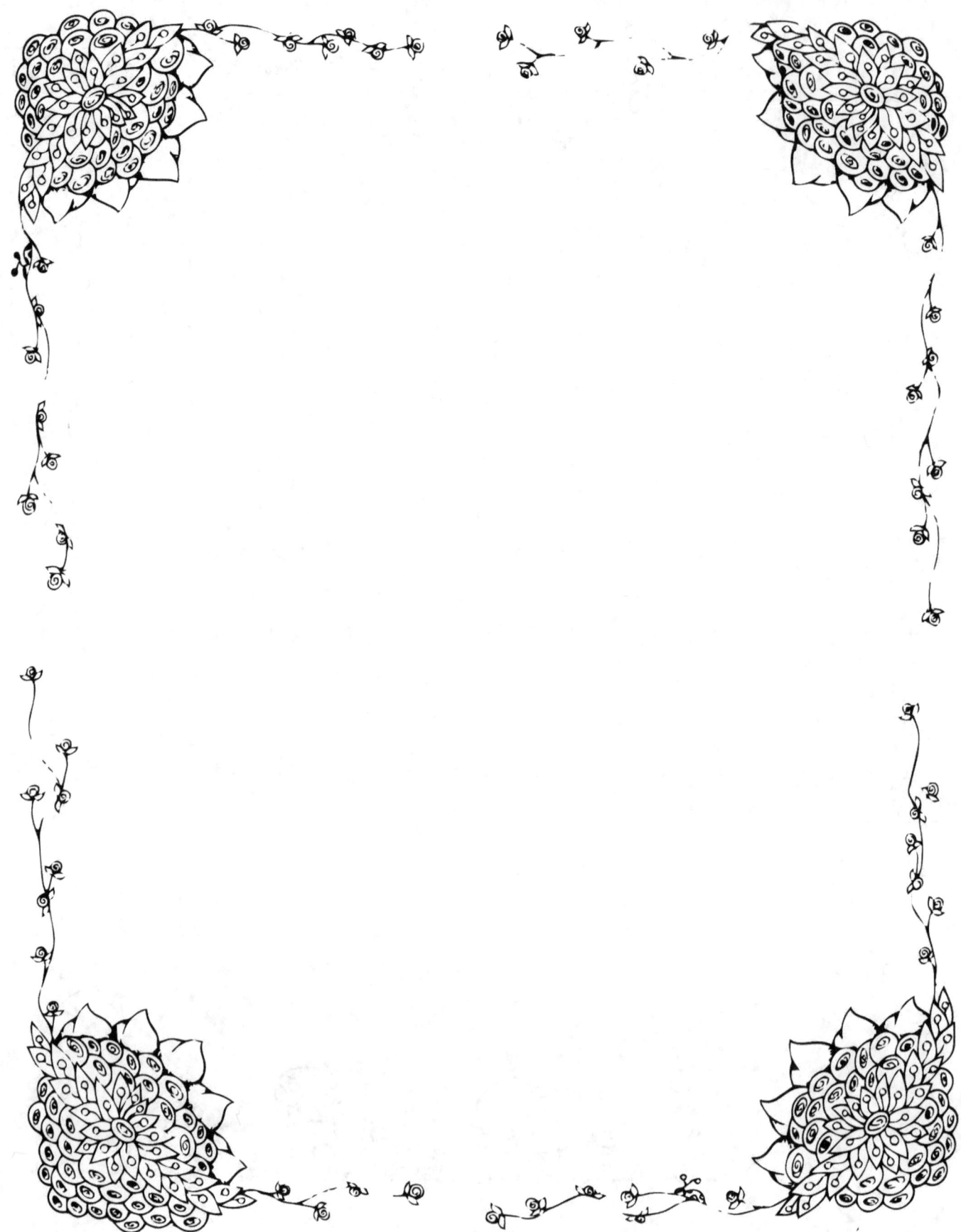

Bonnie S. MacLachlan ©